The 64 Sonnets

The 64 Sonnets

by John Keats

Introduction by Edward Hirsch

Notes by Gary Hawkins

pdb

Paul Dry Books

Philadelphia 2004

First Paul Dry Books Edition, 2004

Paul Dry Books, Inc.
Philadelphia, Pennsylvania
www.pauldrybooks.com

Text type: Granjon
Display type: Poetica
Composed by P. M. Gordon Associates
Designed by Adrianne Onderdonk Dudden

1 3 5 7 9 8 6 4 2
Printed in the United States of America

Library of Congress Cataloging-in-Publication Data

Keats, John, 1795–1821.
[Poems Selections]
The 64 sonnets / John Keats ; introduction by Edward Hirsch ; notes by Gary Hawkins. — 1st Paul Dry Books ed.
p. cm.
ISBN 1-58988-014-5 (trade paper : alk. paper)
1. Sonnets, English. I. Title.

PR4832 2004
821'.7—dc22

2004005036

ISBN 1-58988-014-5

Contents

Keats at Sonnets

by Edward Hirsch

Between 1814 and 1819, John Keats wrote sixty-four sonnets. He was eighteen years old when he composed his first sonnet; he was turning twenty-four when he completed his last one. He restlessly experimented with the fourteen-line form and used it to plunge into (and explore) his emotional depths. You can sit down and read these poems in a single night and have a complete Keatsian experience—he breathes close and offers himself to us; his presence is near. You can also read them throughout your adulthood and never really get to the bottom of them. These short, durable poems are filled with the mysteries of poetry.

In the sonnets, Keats conveys the range of his interests, his concerns, his attachments, his obsessions. Some are light and improvisatory, tossed off in fifteen minutes, a moment's thought. Some are polemics, or romantic period pieces; others are brooding testaments or compulsive outpourings, which seem to expand on the page. These sonnets are replete with a sensuous feeling for nature—"The poetry of earth is never dead"—that looks back to Wordsworth and forward to Frost. They also luxuriate in the spaces of imagination—"Much have I travell'd in the realms of gold"—and trigger the daydreaming capacities of the mind.

Keats came of age in the midst of a full-scale revival of the sonnet form, which had fallen into disfavor and disuse in the latter half of the seventeenth and the first half of the eighteenth centuries. By the time he sat down to write his second known poem, "On Peace" (1814), an irregular or hybrid sonnet celebrating the peace between England and France ("With England's happiness proclaim Europa's liberty"), the sonnet had become a widely used poetic form of the Romantic era. For example, Wordsworth, who looked back to Milton, composed more than five hundred sonnets in his long life. "In sundry moods, 'twas pastime to be bound," he confessed in a sonnet about the sonnet form, "Within the Sonnet's scanty plot of ground."

Keats's first book, *Poems* (1817), comprises a substantial number of sonnets—twenty-one in all. This work shows how vigorously he applied himself to the Petrarchan sonnet, which consists of an octave (*abbaabba*) and a sestet (*cdecde*). The Petrarchan structure invites an asymmetrical division of an argument. It tends to create an obsessive feeling in the first section and then to respond to that feeling—to let it loose—in the second part. It builds the pressure in the first eight lines, turns, and then releases that pressure in the final six lines. Keats was temperamentally drawn to one of the key emotional archetypes of the Petrarchan love sonnet, which creates, as Paul Fussell suggests, "the pattern of sexual pressure and release." He also determined to master the binary structure as a form for meditation, a vessel for internal dialogue and debate.

Keats's self-directed apprenticeship was at least partly conducted under the stimulus of Leigh Hunt, who cultivated the Petrarchan or Italian form. At Enfield School, Keats eagerly absorbed and embraced the liberal principles developed in Hunt's weekly reform-minded newspaper, the *Examiner,* some of which he commemorated in his early sonnet on Hunt's release from prison in 1815. Both Keats and Hunt "sympathized with the lowest commonplace." After they met, in October 1816, Keats wrote three extemporaneous poems in sonnet contests instigated by Hunt: "On the Grasshopper and Cricket," "On Receiving a Laurel Crown from Leigh Hunt," and "To the Nile." In fact, Keats composed a couple of early sonnets—"On Leaving Some Friends at an Early Hour" and "Keen, fitful gusts are whisp'ring here and there"—at Hunt's cottage in the Vale of Health, Hampstead. Hunt's influence on Keats's poetry is evident until 1817.

Charles Cowden Clarke, the son of Keats's schoolmaster and one of his closest friends, tells how Keats wrote out the dedicatory sonnet "To Leigh Hunt, Esq." in one sitting, without a single alteration. "He was surrounded by several of his friends when the last proof-sheet of his little book was brought in; and he was requested to send the dedication, if he intended one. He went to a side-table, and in a few minutes, while all had been talking, he returned and read the Dedicatory Sonnett. . . . The subject of this Sonnett may have lain in the bud of his mind, and had blossomed at his then bidding."

Keats loved the intoxication of creating in a fine frenzy. He believed, as he told his brothers, that "the excellence of every Art is its intensity" (*Letters,* I, no. 45), and the sonnet offered him a form of powerful compactness. He was highly responsive to others—he had a gift for friendship—and his sonnets are filled with addresses and dedications, acknowledgments, literary debts repaid. Friendship was one of his triggering subjects. Love was another. He was also befriended by books, by the great dead who preceded him. He schooled his fluencies. As he concluded in "Keen fitful gusts are whisp'ring here and there":

For I am brimfull of the friendliness
    That in a little cottage I have found;
Of fair-hair'd Milton's eloquent distress,
    And all his love for gentle Lycid drown'd;
Of lovely Laura in her light green dress,
    And faithful Petrarch gloriously crown'd.

Keats was always deeply impressed by imaginative things. He loved to be carried away and overwhelmed, to wander in fictive spaces, secondary worlds. He was a voracious reader with an insatiable appetite for poetry, for Latin authors and mythological keys to classical culture, such as Lemprière's *Classical Dictionary*, Tooke's *Pantheon*, and Spence's *Polymetis*. He felt that his success as a writer, a calling not his by birthright, depended on acquiring material. This unappeasable hunger for books, for ancient stories and myths, for beautiful works of art only increased after he left school at sixteen. He was speaking from personal experience when he called the Grecian urn "a friend to man."

Keats experienced poetry on his pulse. The poems of key predecessors often stimulated his inner life and incited his response. This was certainly the case with his breakthrough sonnet "On first looking into Chapman's Homer," which he wrote at a fever pitch in a couple of enthralling early morning hours in October 1816. This was an emblematic or allegorical moment in Keats's writing life—in the life of any young poet—because his reading vitally seized him and spurred him into his own extravagant making. It fostered his imagination and gave him to himself.

Keats and Cowden Clarke, who was eight years his senior and deeply encouraged his interests, had spent the entire night excitedly poring over a borrowed 1616 folio edition of George Chapman's translation of the *Iliad* and the *Odyssey.* They searched out the magnificent passages, the heart-stopping scenes, and compared Pope's well-tempered eighteenth-century couplets with Chapman's more propulsive, free-striding Elizabethan verse. Keats tore himself away at six in the morning. He departed "at day-spring," as Clarke later recalled, "yet he contrived that I should receive the poem, from a distance of nearly two miles, before 10 a.m." A fair copy of the poem was sitting on Clarke's table when he came down to breakfast. (In the right-hand margin of the manuscript, Keats drew lines to mark the rhyme scheme for the octave of the Petrarchan sonnet, a form he knew well, which suggests that he was composing rapidly and also plainly tired after such a memorable night.)

Keats's sonnet enacts a feeling of rapturous discovery; it breathes its own wonderment. It creates the sensation of tremendous vastness within the prescribed space of the Petrarchan form. The twenty-year-old poet builds his case so convincingly that readers ever after have been powerfully affected by the swelling turn in the sonnet, the reverberations of the final sestet. Only when he heard Chapman's bold rendition of "deep-brow'd Homer," the speaker reveals:

> Then felt I like some watcher of the skies
>   When a new planet swims into his ken;
> Or like stout Cortez when with eagle eyes
>   He star'd at the Pacific—and all his men
> Look'd at each other with a wild surmise—
>   Silent, upon a peak in Darien.

Keats's sonnet "completely announced the new poet taking possession," as Hunt put it. It is his first major work. Yet there is also a touching way that Keats reveals himself to be a newcomer to high culture. He implicitly acknowledges that he doesn't read Homer in the original Greek, that he is just now coming upon Chapman's translation: "On *first* looking . . ." (In a later sonnet entitled "To Homer," he refers to his own "giant ignorance.") So, too, he mistakes Balboa for Cortez, as Tennyson first pointed out to Palgrave. But what matters more deeply is the rising excitement and sense of limitless possibility created in him by reading Homer, so that he feels poised on the brink of a great discovery, like Herschel finding the planet Uranus or Balboa suddenly sighting the Pacific Ocean. Reading Homer, even in translation, Keats enters a fabulous new world. He, too, ascends into a space of silent awe, and he instills that same feeling in us.

Some critics have worried that Keats's aspirations to high culture are somehow suspect, but I believe they have an almost Blakean political dignity. They speak to what we all might gain access to, what we would joyously create within ourselves. Chapman's Homer becomes Keats's method of transport, his way of joining with "the mighty dead" (*Endymion*), attaining the sublime. He had found a means for declaring, possessing, and authoring himself.

Keats was actively taken—almost physically seized—by art and often pulled into the visual realm of paintings, engravings, and sculptures. The character of high art—what had previously been made great—could be both energizing and daunting to him. It could have forbidding power. One thinks, for example, of that day in the winter of 1817 when Keats's older friend, the historical painter Benjamin Haydon, took him to see the Parthenon sculptures being exhibited for the first time at the British Museum. Keats's visceral response must have surprised Haydon, for instead of being intoxicated by the splendor, as the painter fully expected, the poet was dazed and silenced by what he saw. Keats had received the first copy of his *Poems* just a day or two earlier, and it seems to me that the excitement—and the shock—must have heightened his museum experience and contributed to his overpowering encounter. The magnificence of the Elgin Marbles brought home to him that there was an enormous gap, a palpable abyss, between what he hoped to do and what he had actually accomplished. He took the greatness of the statues personally, almost competitively.

The sonnet "On Seeing the Elgin Marbles" dramatizes Keats's experience of speechless astonishment. The passage of time counterpoised against the immutable splendor of Grecian art induced in him a dizzying panic, a debilitating vertigo. He could but dimly apprehend the magnitude he was seeking. Yet he had already begun to apprentice himself to what he called "the religion of Joy," the Greek spirit made flesh. I suspect he was steeling himself for a fresh start, for what the poem deems "godlike hardship," for the great work to come. The threat of failure could overwhelm Keats, as in his dirge-like sonnet "When I have fears that I may cease to be," but he ultimately responded by rededicating himself to the creative task with a deeper candor, a more furious resolve.

Keats wrote his sonnets in a wide variety of moods: with affection, with disgust, with outrage, with embarrassment, with passionate longing. They have a mortal stamp and increasingly take on a tragic grandeur. He conceived his early sonnets under the spell of Spenserian romance, his later ones under the sign of Shakespearean tragedy. Keats wrote much of his long poem *Endymion* (1818), which can been seen as a dividing line, under the aspiring dream—the phantasm—of Shakespeare. ("Is it too daring to Fancy Shakspeare this Presider?" he queried Haydon, *Letters,* I, no. 26.) "I never quite despair and I read Shakspeare—indeed I shall I think never read any other Book much," Keats declared in the same letter. "I am very near Agreeing with Hazlitt that Shakspeare is enough for us" (*Letters,* I, no. 26).

In his well-known *Lectures on the English Poets,* William Hazlitt argued that Shakespeare "was the least of an egotist that it was possible to be. He was nothing in himself; but he was all that others were, or that they could become." Keats was galvanized by Hazlitt's notion that Shakespeare "had only to think of any thing in order to become that thing, with all the circumstances belonging to it." Keats read Shakespeare's sonnets with great avidity ("I neer found so many beauties in the sonnets—they seem to be full of fine things said unintentionally," he wrote to J. H. Reynolds in November 1817, *Letters,* I, no. 44) and adapted what he read. Largely from reading and imitating Shakespeare, Keats came to understand and theorize ductility as an essential feature of artistic imagination. He hypothesized that the human imagination at its most receptive is saturated with what, in a letter to his brothers, he famously called "Negative Capability."

> *Negative Capability,* that is when man is capable of being in uncertainties, Mysteries, doubts, without any irritable reaching after fact & reason (*Letters,* I, no. 45).

For Keats, the displacement of the poet's protean self into another existence was the key feature of the highest poetic imagination. He believed that this heightened receptivity was part of the native genius of English poetry. He explained his ideal of the self-annulling poetic character more fully in a letter to Richard Woodhouse in October 1818:

> As to the poetical Character itself . . . it is not itself—it has no self—it is every thing and nothing—It has no character—it enjoys light and shade; it lives in gusto, be it foul or fair, high or low, rich or poor, mean or elevated—It has as much delight in conceiving an Iago as an Imogen. What shocks the virtuous philosop[h]er, delights the camelion Poet. . . . A Poet is the most unpoetical of any thing in existence; because he has no Identity—he is continually in for—and filling some other Body—The Sun, the Moon, the Sea and Men and Women who are creatures of impulse are poetical and have about them an unchangeable attribute—the poet has none; no identity (*Letters,* I, no. 118).

Recently, Helen Vendler has written that after Keats dissociated himself from Hunt ("It is a great Pity that People should by associating themselves with the fine[st] things, spoil them—Hunt has damned Hampstead [and] Masks and Sonnets and italian tales," he wrote to Haydon in 1818, *Letters,* I, no. 70), he adopted "Shakespearean tragic values" and the Shakespearean sonnet as a "vehicle of choice." Keats used the highly reasonable, toughly reasoning Shakespearean sonnet (three quatrains and a couplet: *abab, cdcd, efef, gg)* to powerful effect. He created wild disturbances within the well-balanced, predetermined form.

I agree with Vendler that the precise turning point in Keats's changeover is "On Sitting Down to Read *King Lear* Once Again," which he wrote while he was preparing *Endymion* for press. "I think a little change has taken place in my intellect lately," Keats announced to his brothers:

> Nothing is finer for the purposes of great productions, than a very gradual ripening of the intellectual powers—As an instance of this—observe—I sat down yesterday to read King Lear once again the thing appeared to demand the prologue of a Sonnet, I wrote it & began to read (*Letters,* I, no. 56).

"On Sitting Down to Read *King Lear* Once Again" employs a hybrid form. Keats uses the opening lines of a Petrarchan octave to bid farewell to the seductive female muse of the Romance mode:

> O golden-tongued Romance, with serene lute!
> Fair plumed syren, queen of far-away!
> Leave melodizing on this wintry day,
> Shut up thine olden pages, and be mute.
> Adieu!

In the last six lines of the poem, he employs a Shakespearean pattern to address the male poet who had become his supreme model:

> Chief Poet! and ye clouds of Albion,
>   Begetters of our deep eternal theme!
> When through the old oak forest I am gone,
>   Let me not wander in a barren dream:
> But, when I am consumed in the fire,
> Give me new Phoenix wings to fly at my desire.

Walter Jackson Bate suggests that the poems in which Keats goes on to use the Shakespearean or English pattern are "the most truly Shakespearean sonnets of the nineteenth (or, for that matter, twentieth) century, whether in metrical variation, pause, quatrain division, or even rhetorical devices."

Throughout his late work, Keats invokes the redeeming powers of consciousness. He takes up "the fierce dispute / Betwixt damnation and impassion'd clay"; he tastes "the bitter-sweet of this Shakespearean fruit" ("On Sitting Down to Read *King Lear* Once Again"). His three greatest Shakespearean sonnets, "When I have fears that I may cease to be," "Why did I laugh tonight? No voice will tell," and "Bright star, would I were stedfast as thou art," bear the excruciating weight of mortality, of a nearly unbearable passion. They are filled with presentiments of death. In one of his last poetic acts Keats copied "Bright star" onto a blank page in Severn's volume of Shakespeare during their final voyage to Italy. The end of

"Why did I laugh tonight?" shows how illness preyed on his feverishly active consciousness, how the thought of fast-approaching death could paralyze even his three deepest impulses and longings:

> Why did I laugh? I know this being's lease—
> My fancy to its utmost blisses spreads:
> Yet could I on this very midnight cease,
> And the world's gaudy ensigns see in shreds.
> Verse, fame, and beauty are intense indeed,
> But death intenser—death is Life's high meed.

Keats returned to the Shakespearean form in his final two sonnets, written in "wretched thrall" to his fiancée Fanny Brawne, who was the object of his obsessive, nearly overwhelming passion. "Love is my religion—I could die for that," he wrote to her. "My Creed is Love and you are its only tenet—You have ravish'd me away by a Power I cannot resist; and yet I could resist till I saw you; and even since I have seen you I have endeavoured often 'to reason against the reasons of my Love'" (*Letters,* II, no. 203). Keats's emotional distress is palpable in his last sonnets where the closely reasoned form, the calculated incisiveness, works exceptionally well for his highly unreasonable, tormented subject.

Even as he was composing the major odes that are the high-water mark of his work, Keats continued experimenting with the sonnet form. In a short period, he wrote four sonnets that remarkably test and experiment with sonnet structure: "Sonnet to Sleep"; "On Fame" (I and II);

and "If by dull rhymes our English must be chain'd," which is a formal directive, an *ars poetica.* "I have been endeavouring to discover a better sonnet stanza than we have," he wrote in a letter to George and Georgiana Keats in which he enclosed a copy of "If by dull rhymes." "The legitimate [Petrarchan sonnet] does not suit the language over-well from the pouncing rhymes—the other kind [the Shakespearean sonnet] appears too elegaic [*sic*]" (*Letters,* II, no. 159). Thus he was determined to avoid these effects and to "find out, if we must be constrain'd, / Sandals more interwoven and complete / To fit the naked foot of Poesy."

Keats's quest for a more malleable sonnet form also led him to create the stately ten-line stanza of the great odes. He grafted a Shakespearean quatrain (*abab*) onto a Petrarchan sestet (*cdecde*), and thus established the fundamental pattern for four central poems: "Ode to a Nightingale," "Ode on a Grecian Urn," "Ode on Melancholy," and "Ode on Indolence." Keats used the pattern to maintain the "interwoven and complete" character of the sonnet—each stanza is a fully integrated unit—while also weaving the sections into a whole. Thus the capaciousness of the odes was made possible by his persistent experimentation with the sonnet form.

Here, then, are sixty-four sonnets—at once a major accomplishment and an intimate and approachable body of work by one of the great poets of sympathetic absorption, a writer who believed in the "holiness of the Heart's affections and the truth of Imagination" (*Letters,* I, no. 43).

These fourteen-line poems deliver us to ourselves more fully and more wholly, through the sensuous, rhythmic, musical language of attainment. Keats discovered that the sonnet is a small vessel capable of plunging tremendous depths. It is one of the enabling forms of human inwardness. We are befriended by these passionate, wayward, adventurous poems. Indeed, we are befriended by art itself, Keats teaches us, in our struggle with ourselves, in our urgent soul-making. We are made more human and noble by reading him, for he is a hero of our jubilant, flawed, tragic humanity.

Notes to Introduction

Keats's letters are cited from *The Letters of John Keats: 1814–1821,* ed. Hyder Edward Rollins, 2 volumes (Cambridge: Harvard University Press, 1958). They are abbreviated in the introduction as *Letters,* followed by volume and letter number.

ix *sixty-four sonnets:* Helen Vendler presents a table of sixty-four sonnets written by Keats, with dates of composition and first publication, in *Coming of Age as a Poet: Milton, Keats, Eliot, Plath* (Cambridge: Harvard University Press, 2003), 71–79. We follow her numbering. (See Appendix, p. 135.)

x *"In sundry moods . . .":* Wordsworth's poem ("Nuns fret not at their Convent's narrow room") was called "Prefatory Sonnet" and headed a series of sonnets. See William Wordsworth, *Poems, In Two Volumes, and Other Poems, 1800–1807,* ed. Jared Curtis (Ithaca: Cornell University Press, 1983), 133.

x *"the pattern of sexual pressure . . .":* Paul Fussell, Jr., *Poetic Meter and Poetic Form* (New York: Random House, 1965), 121.

xi *who cultivated the Petrarchan . . . :* Leigh Hunt considered the Petrarchan form "the Sonnet Proper, or what is called the Legitimate Sonnet." He advocated for the Italian form, considered the freer Shakespearean pattern "unartistical," and especially disliked the interlacing Spenserian type (*abab, bcbc, cdcd, ee*). "The rhyme scheme seems at once less responsive and always interfering," he wrote, "and the music has no longer its major and minor divisions." Hunt's opinion may have had a decisive influence on Keats who, despite his great love for Spenser, seems never to have flirted with the Spenserian form. See Leigh Hunt, "An Essay on the Cultivation, History, and Variety of Poem Called the Sonnet" (1867). *Selected Writings of Leigh Hunt,* volume 4, ed. Charles Mahoney (London: Pickering and Chatto, 2003), 291–320.

xi *"sympathized with the lowest commonplace":* Hunt's phrase is quoted in John Barnard, *John Keats* (New York: Cambridge University Press, 1987), 136.

xi *Charles Cowden Clarke, the son . . . : The Keats Circle: Letters and Papers,* 1816–1878, ed. Hyder Edward Rollins, 2 vols. (Cambridge, Mass., 1948). Cited in Jack Stillinger, *Complete Poems*, p. 428. Clarke gives a detailed account in Charles and Mary Cowden Clarke, *Recollections of Writers* (New York: C. Scribner's Sons, 1878), 137–138.

xii *addresses and dedications:* Lawrence John Zillman presents a table of the principle themes in Keats's sonnets in his 1939 work, *John Keats and the Sonnet Tradition: A Critical and Comparative Study* (New York: Octagon Books, 1966), 84. For example, Zillman notes that Keats addressed two poems to his brothers, four to Benjamin Haydon, three to John Hamilton Reynolds, one to Charles Wells, and one to Georgiana Augusta Wylie. He addressed poems to Burns, Byron, Chapman, Chatteron, Coleridge, Homer, Hunt, Milton, Petrarch, Sappho, Scott, Shakespeare, Spenser, and Wordsworth. Zillman counts two sonnets on cities, three on humanity, four on art, five on friendship, seven on fame, seven more on the pleasures of poetry, and so forth.

xiii *He departed "at day-spring . . .":* Charles Cowden Clarke describes the circumstances in *Recollections of Writers*, 128–130.

xiv *"completely announced . . .":* Leigh Hunt, *Lord Byron and Some of His Contemporaries* (London: H. Colburn, 1828), 248.

xvi *"the religion of Joy":* Andrew Motion, *Keats* (New York: Farrar, Straus and Giroux, 1998), 151.

xvii *In his well-known* Lectures *. . . :* William Hazlitt, *Lectures on the English Poets.* Third edition, edited by his son. (1841; New York: Russell and Russell, 1968), 88, 89.

xviii *Helen Vendler has written . . . : Coming of Age as a Poet,* 44–45

xix *the precise turning point . . . :* Vendler, ibid., 62–63.

xx *"the most truly Shakespearean . . .":* Walter Jackson Bate, *John Keats* (Cambridge: Belknap Press of Harvard University Press, 1963), 299.

The 64 Sonnets

No. 1. Possibly written in 1814, as suggested by its subject (see note to line 1).

First published in *Notes and Queries* on February 4, 1905.

1 *Oh Peace!:* Napoleon abdicated the throne in April 1814 and the peaceful Hundred Days followed.

2 *this war-surrounded isle:* Britain

4 *triple kingdom:* Great Britain, composed of England, Scotland, and Wales

8 *sweet mountain nymph:* In *L'Allegro,* English poet John Milton calls to one of the three Graces, "And in thy right hand lead with thee, / The Mountain Nymph, sweet Liberty."

9 *Europa:* Europe. Europa is a beautiful Phoenician princess who attracts the lustful attention of Zeus. The god changes himself into a magnificent white bull to lure the girl onto his back. He then carries her across the sea to Crete.

10 *sceptred tyrants:* Although tyrannical ambitions may have existed among the Jacobins and Napoleon, the rulers who would keep Europe in her pre-Revolutionary "former state" were the Bourbon monarchs whose dynasty was reinstated following the surrender of Napoleon.

12 *thy chains burst:* French philosopher Jean-Jacques Rousseau heralded the French Revolution in his *Social Contract* with the opening lines: "Man is born free; and everywhere he is in chains."

13 *thy kings law:* Louis XVIII, who ascended to the throne in 1814, kept most of Napoleon's bureaucracy intact.

14 *the horrors past:* the French Revolution's Reign of Terror, 1793–94

On Peace

Oh Peace! and dost thou with thy presence bless
    The dwellings of this war-surrounded isle;
Soothing with placid brow our late distress,
4   Making the triple kingdom brightly smile?
Joyful I hail thy presence; and I hail
    The sweet companions that await on thee;
Complete my joy—let not my first wish fail,
8   Let the sweet mountain nymph thy favorite be,
With England's happiness proclaim Europa's liberty.
Oh Europe, let not sceptred tyrants see
    That thou must shelter in thy former state;
12 Keep thy chains burst, and boldly say thou art free;
    Give thy kings law—leave not uncurbed the great;
    So with the horrors past thou'lt win thy happier fate.

No. 2. Written in December 1814. Richard Woodhouse, chief transcriber of Keats's work, included a note with one of his copies of the Keats manuscript which reported that Keats had said "he had written it on the death of his grandmother, about five days afterward, but that he had never told any one before (not even his brother) the occasion upon which it was written. He said he was tenderly attached to her."

First published in *The Poetical Works of John Keats* (1876).

3 *pinions:* wings
nought: naught
6 *circlets:* halos
7 *bedight:* arrayed
9 *quire:* choir
12 *cleavest:* split

As from the darkening gloom a silver dove

As from the darkening gloom a silver dove
    Upsoars, and darts into the eastern light,
    On pinions that nought moves but pure delight;
4 So fled thy soul into the realms above,
Regions of peace and everlasting love;
    Where happy spirits, crowned with circlets bright
    Of starry beam, and gloriously bedight,
8 Taste the high joy none but the bless'd can prove.
There thou or joinest the immortal quire
    In melodies that even heaven fair
Fill with superior bliss, or, at desire
12 Of the omnipotent Father, cleavest the air,
On holy message sent.—What pleasures higher?
    Wherefore does any grief our joy impair?

No. 3. Written in December 1814. Lord Byron (1788–1824) was a strikingly handsome contemporary of Keats who remarked after the publication of his *Childe Harold's Pilgrimage:* "I awoke to find myself famous." The two poets—one a successful nobleman and one an obscure member of the working class—became rivals, and Byron was among those who disparaged Keats as a member of the "Cockney School" of common poetry. Later, in his elegy, *Adonais,* the poet Shelley (1792–1822) blames Keats's death on "the wound which his sensitive spirit had received from the criticism." Byron responded in a canto of *Don Juan:* "Poor fellow! His was an untoward fate:— / 'Tis strange the mind, that very fiery particle, / Should let itself be snuffed out by an Article."

First published in *Life, Letters, and Literary Remains of John Keats* (1848).

1 *Byron . . . thy melody:* The Byronic hero is a bold but melancholy wanderer in constant search of love.

3 *Pity:* Melopemene, the Muse of tragedy who nonetheless sang joyously

4 *by:* near

To Lord Byron

Byron, how sweetly sad thy melody,
 Attuning still the soul to tenderness,
 As if soft Pity with unusual stress
4 Had touch'd her plaintive lute; and thou, being by,
Hadst caught the tones, nor suffered them to die.
 O'ershading sorrow doth not make thee less
 Delightful: thou thy griefs dost dress
8 With a bright halo, shining beamily;
As when a cloud a golden moon doth veil,
 Its sides are tinged with a resplendent glow,
Through the dark robe oft amber rays prevail,
12 And like fair veins in sable marble flow.
Still warble, dying swan,—still tell the tale,
 The enchanting tale—the tale of pleasing woe.

No. 4. Written in 1815. Thomas Chatterton (1752–1770) was a prodigy born into a poor family in Bristol, England. By the age of twelve, he was composing his own works and passing them off as the "Rowley Poems," claiming they were copies of fifteenth-century manuscripts. After the ruse was discovered, he moved to London where he met with little success. Facing starvation, Chatterton poisoned himself at the age of seventeen. His tragedy was idealized by Keats and other Romantics. Keats dedicated *Endymion* to Chatterton: "Inscribed To The Memory Of Thomas Chatterton."

First published in *Life, Letters, and Literary Remains of John Keats* (1848).

5 *elate:* elated
8 *amate:* overwhelm
10 *spheres:* heavens

Oh Chatterton! how very sad thy fate

Oh Chatterton! how very sad thy fate!
    Dear child of sorrow! son of misery!
    How soon the film of death obscur'd that eye,
4 Whence genius wildly flash'd, and high debate!
How soon that voice, majestic and elate,
    Melted in dying murmurs! O how nigh
    Was night to thy fair morning! Thou didst die
8 A half-blown flower, which cold blasts amate.
But this is past. Thou art among the stars
    Of highest heaven; to the rolling spheres
Thou sweetly singest—nought thy hymning mars
12 Above the ingrate world and human fears.
On earth the good man base detraction bars
    From thy fair name, and waters it with tears!

No. 5. Written on February 2, 1815. In his *Recollections of Writers,* Keats's friend Charles Cowden Clarke (1787–1877) recalls walking that day toward Horsemonger Lane Prison from which the poet Leigh Hunt (1784–1859) had just been released after serving a two-year sentence for "unwise libel upon the Prince Regent." Clarke met Keats returning from the prison, and when they parted Keats handed him a copy of the sonnet composed that very day. Keats had previously kept the fact of his writing a secret to both family and friends, and so for Clarke that was "the first proof I had received of his having committed himself in verse; and how clearly do I recall the conscious look and hesitation with which he offered it!"

First published in *Poems* (1817).

4 *lark:* A bird known to sing in mid-flight, the lark is a popular figure for poets, e.g., Shelley's "To a Sky-Lark," in which the poet aspires to the lark's "profuse strains of unpremeditated art."

5 *minion:* a servant or sycophant

9 *Spenser:* English poet (1552?–1599) whose *The Faerie Queen* inspired Keats with both its epic aspirations and stylistic innovations. Keats heads his first book of poems with a likeness of Spenser and a quotation: "What more felicity can fall to creature / Then to enjoy delight with liberty."

bowers: shady places of retreat or seclusion

11 *daring Milton:* English poet John Milton's (1608–74) epic *Paradise Lost* was an early Protestant challenge to traditional Christian beliefs and intends to "justify the ways of God to man."

Written on the Day That Mr. Leigh Hunt Left Prison

What though, for showing truth to flatter'd state,
    Kind Hunt was shut in prison, yet has he,
    In his immortal spirit, been as free
4 As the sky-searching lark, and as elate.
Minion of grandeur! think you he did wait?
    Think you he nought but prison walls did see,
    Till, so unwilling, thou unturn'dst the key?
8 Ah, no! far happier, nobler was his fate!
In Spenser's halls he strayed, and bowers fair,
    Culling enchanted flowers; and he flew
With daring Milton through the fields of air:
12   To regions of his own his genius true
Took happy flights. Who shall his fame impair
    When thou art dead, and all thy wretched crew?

No. 6. Written in 1815 or 1816. This poem and the two which follow were composed as a triple sonnet.

First published in *Poems* (1817).

2 *fancies:* As Coleridge (1772–1834) defines it, fancy—full of "fixities and definites"—is a lesser faculty than imagination, that creative and transmuting power of the poet.

12 *Calidore:* The hero of Book VI of Spenser's *The Faerie Queen* strives for triumph via the virtue of Courtesy. In his own unfinished poem "Calidore," Keats describes the knight's "healthful spirit eager and awake / To feel the beauty of a silent eve."

13 *Red Cross Knight:* The hero of Book I of *The Faerie Queen* quests toward Holiness.

Leander: The youth who swims the Hellespont every night to be with his beloved Hero. One night in a storm, he loses sight of the beacon that Hero lights for him, and he perishes in the strait. When his body washes onto shore, Hero throws herself from her watchtower in grief.

Woman! when I behold thee flippant, vain

Woman! when I behold thee flippant, vain,
    Inconstant, childish, proud, and full of fancies;
    Without that modest softening that enhances
4 The downcast eye, repentant of the pain
That its mild light creates to heal again:
    E'en then, elate, my spirit leaps, and prances,
    E'en then my soul with exultation dances
8 For that to love, so long, I've dormant lain:
But when I see thee meek, and kind, and tender,
    Heavens! how desperately do I adore
Thy winning graces;—to be thy defender
12   I hotly burn—to be a Calidore—
A very Red Cross Knight—a stout Leander—
    Might I be loved by thee like these of yore.

No. 7. Written in 1815 or 1816 as the second part of a triple sonnet. First published in *Poems* (1817).

9 *lark:* a whim, a carelessness

12 *intelligences:* In an 1819 letter, Keats writes of "Soul as distinguished from an Intelligence—There may be intelligences or sparks of the divinity in millions—but they are not Souls till they acquire identities, till each one is personally itself."

Light feet, dark violet eyes, and parted hair

Light feet, dark violet eyes, and parted hair;
    Soft dimpled hands, white neck, and creamy breast,
    Are things on which the dazzled senses rest
4 Till the fond, fixed eyes forget they stare.
From such fine pictures, heavens! I cannot dare
    To turn my admiration, though unpossess'd
    They be of what is worthy,—though not drest
8 In lovely modesty, and virtues rare.
Yet these I leave as thoughtless as a lark;
    These lures I straight forget,—e'en ere I dine,
Or thrice my palate moisten: but when I mark
12 Such charms with mild intelligences shine,
My ear is open like a greedy shark,
    To catch the tunings of a voice divine.

No. 8. Written in 1815 or 1816 as the third part of a triple sonnet. First published in *Poems* (1817).

4 *All-seeing:* God
6 *pinions:* wings
intreats: entreats, requests
10 *lay:* song, as played on an instrument

Ah! who can e'er forget so fair a being

Ah! who can e'er forget so fair a being?
    Who can forget her half retiring sweets?
    God! she is like a milk-white lamb that bleats
4 For man's protection. Surely the All-seeing,
Who joys to see us with his gifts agreeing,
    Will never give him pinions, who intreats
    Such innocence to ruin,—who vilely cheats
8 A dove-like bosom. In truth there is no freeing
One's thoughts from such a beauty; when I hear
    A lay that once I saw her hand awake,
Her form seems floating palpable, and near;
12 Had I e'er seen her from an arbour take
A dewy flower, oft would that hand appear,
    And o'er my eyes the trembling moisture shake.

No. 9. Written in 1815 or 1816.

First published in Leigh Hunt's *Examiner* on May 5, 1816, it was Keats's first work to be published. Included in *Poems* (1817).

2–3 *jumbled heap of murky buildings:* In 1815, Keats moved from rural Edmonton to the London borough of Southwark, a locale which he described as "a beastly place in dirt, turnings and windings." Here he would be near Guy's Hospital where he soon began his study of medicine.

3 *steep:* a precipitous slope

6 *span:* the distance from the tip of the thumb to the tip of the little finger, i.e., a relatively short distance

8 *fox-glove bell:* a common English wildflower with downward-hanging, bell-shaped blooms

O Solitude! if I must with thee dwell

O Solitude! if I must with thee dwell,
    Let it not be among the jumbled heap
    Of murky buildings; climb with me the steep,—
4 Nature's observatory—whence the dell,
Its flowery slopes, its river's crystal swell,
    May seem a span; let me thy vigils keep
    'Mongst boughs pavillion'd, where the deer's swift leap
8 Startles the wild bee from the fox-glove bell.
But though I'll gladly trace these scenes with thee,
    Yet the sweet converse of an innocent mind,
    Whose words are images of thoughts refin'd,
12 Is my soul's pleasure; and it sure must be
    Almost the highest bliss of human-kind,
When to thy haunts two kindred spirits flee.

No. 10. Written in 1815 or 1816.

First published in *Poems* (1817) with the title "To * * * * * *," whose identity has never been determined.

1 *fair:* unblemished, suitable
6 *cuirass:* breastplate
10 *Hybla:* an ancient, highland city in Sicily known to the Greeks as a divine garden and source of the nectar of the gods
12 *meet:* fitting, fair

Had I a man's fair form, then might my sighs

Had I a man's fair form, then might my sighs
    Be echoed swiftly through that ivory shell
    Thine ear, and find thy gentle heart; so well
4 Would passion arm me for the enterprize:
But ah! I am no knight whose foeman dies;
    No cuirass glistens on my bosom's swell;
    I am no happy shepherd of the dell
8 Whose lips have trembled with a maiden's eyes.
Yet must I dote upon thee,—call thee sweet,
    Sweeter by far than Hybla's honied roses
        When steep'd in dew rich to intoxication.
12 Ah! I will taste that dew, for me 'tis meet,
    And when the moon her pallid face discloses,
        I'll gather some by spells, and incantation.

No. 11. Written in June 1816.
First published in *Poems* (1817).

1 *To one . . . in city pent:* a reference to Milton's *Paradise Lost* (Book IX, 445–8): "As one who long in populous city pent . . . breathe[s] / Among the pleasant villages and farms."
pent: pent-up, confined

7–8 *a debonair . . . languishment:* a reference to Leigh Hunt's romance *The Story of Rimini,* which was published in 1816

10 *Philomel:* a nightingale. Philomela is raped by her brother-in-law, Tereus, who cuts out the girl's tongue to keep her from revealing the deed. After avenging this act with the aid of her sister, Procne, and while trying to flee the wrathful Tereus, Philomela is transformed into a nightingale, acquiring the bird's rich song.

11 *career:* a course through the sky

14 *ether:* the heavens

To one who has been long in city pent

To one who has been long in city pent,
    'Tis very sweet to look into the fair
    And open face of heaven,—to breathe a prayer
4 Full in the smile of the blue firmament.
Who is more happy, when, with heart's content,
    Fatigued he sinks into some pleasant lair
    Of wavy grass, and reads a debonair
8 And gentle tale of love and languishment?
Returning home at evening, with an ear
    Catching the notes of Philomel,—an eye
Watching the sailing cloudlet's bright career,
12   He mourns that day so soon has glided by:
E'en like the passage of an angel's tear
    That falls through the clear ether silently.

No. 12. Written in 1816.

First published in *Life, Letters, and Literary Remains of John Keats* (1848).

3 *zephyrs:* light breezes

5 *meaner:* more unpleasant, or more moderate

7 *fragrant wild:* a wilderness

9 *patriotic lore:* the English tradition of poetry. Keats remarked in a letter, "I think I shall be among the English Poets."

10 *Sydney:* Algernon Sydney (1622–83), English politician opposed to the restoration of Charles I and executed for treason. He is also mentioned in Keats's "Lines written on May 29, the Anniversary of Charles's Restoration, on Hearing the Bells Ringing."

bier: frame used to carry a coffin to a graveside

14 *spells:* enchants, or relieves

Oh! how I love, on a fair summer's eve

Oh! how I love, on a fair summer's eve,
  When streams of light pour down the golden west,
  And on the balmy zephyrs tranquil rest
4 The silver clouds, far—far away to leave
All meaner thoughts, and take a sweet reprieve
  From little cares:—to find, with easy quest,
  A fragrant wild, with Nature's beauty drest,
8 And there into delight my soul deceive.
There warm my breast with patriotic lore,
  Musing on Milton's fate—on Sydney's bier—
    Till their stern forms before my mind arise:
12 Perhaps on the wing of poesy upsoar,—
  Full often dropping a delicious tear,
    When some melodious sorrow spells mine eyes.

No. 13. Written on June 29, 1816. The poet (and practical joker) Charles Jeremiah Wells (1800–79) was the "friend" who sent Keats the roses, either as a prank or to end a previous quarrel.

First published in *Poems* (1817).

1 *happy fields:* from Milton's *Paradise Lost* (Book I, 249–50): "Farewell happy fields, / Where joy forever dwells: hail, horrors!"

3 *covert:* underbrush, cover

6 *musk-rose:* fragrant, wild rose shrub with strongly fragrant blooms; cf. Keats's "Ode To a Nightingale": "mid-May's eldest child, / The coming musk-rose, full of dewy wine."

8 *Titania:* in folklore, queen of the fairies or, like Diana, goddess-queen of the nymphs

11 *Wells:* Charles Jeremiah Wells (see above)

To a Friend Who Sent Me Some Roses

As late I rambled in the happy fields,
  What time the sky-lark shakes the tremulous dew
  From his lush clover covert;—when anew
4 Adventurous knights take up their dinted shields:
I saw the sweetest flower wild nature yields,
  A fresh-blown musk-rose; 'twas the first that threw
  Its sweets upon the summer: graceful it grew
8 As is the wand that queen Titania wields.
And, as I feasted on its fragrancy,
  I thought the garden-rose it far excell'd:
But when, O Wells! thy roses came to me
12 My sense with their deliciousness was spell'd:
Soft voices had they, that with tender plea
  Whisper'd of peace, and truth, and friendliness unquell'd.

No. 14. Possibly written in 1816.
First published in *Poems* (1817).

2 *verdure:* greenery, abundant growth
4 *high romances:* tales of chivalrous journey and conquest
blent: blended
8 *worldling:* a person absorbed with earthly desires
9 *artless daughters:* Scotland and Wales
13 *glance:* luster

Happy is England! I could be content

Happy is England! I could be content
    To see no other verdure than its own;
    To feel no other breezes than are blown
4 Through its tall woods with high romances blent:
Yet do I sometimes feel a languishment
    For skies Italian, and an inward groan
    To sit upon an Alp as on a throne,
8 And half forget what world or worldling meant.
Happy is England, sweet her artless daughters;
    Enough their simple loveliness for me,
        Enough their whitest arms in silence clinging:
12 Yet do I often warmly burn to see
        Beauties of deeper glance, and hear their singing,
And float with them about the summer waters.

No. 15. Written in August 1816. Having completed his apothecary exams in July, Keats went to the town of Margate, on the coast, where he composed this poem to George (1797–1841).

First published in *Poems* (1817).

2 *kist:* kissed

3–4 *laurel'd peers . . . lean:* the sunset, the rays of which are the distinctive fellows of the sunrise (hence, "laurelled peers")

10 *Cynthia:* the Virgin Moon. She enchants the shepherd-hero of Keats's long poem, *Endymion.*

silken curtains: the clouds

To My Brother George

Many the wonders I this day have seen:
    The sun, when first he kist away the tears
    That fill'd the eyes of morn;—the laurel'd peers
4 Who from the feathery gold of evening lean;—
The ocean with its vastness, its blue green,
    Its ships, its rocks, its caves, its hopes, its fears,—
    Its voice mysterious, which whoso hears
8 Must think on what will be, and what has been.
E'en now, dear George, while this for you I write,
    Cynthia is from her silken curtains peeping
So scantly, that it seems her bridal night,
12   And she her half-discover'd revels keeping.
But what, without the social thought of thee,
Would be the wonders of the sky and sea?

No. 16. Possibly written in 1816.
First published in *Poems* (1817).

1 *bards:* poets, i.e., Keats's predecessors
2 *A few of them:* namely, the epic poets Milton and Spenser
4 *sublime:* awesome, divine

How many bards gild the lapses of time

How many bards gild the lapses of time!
    A few of them have ever been the food
    Of my delighted fancy,—I could brood
4 Over their beauties, earthly, or sublime:
And often, when I sit me down to rhyme,
    These will in throngs before my mind intrude:
    But no confusion, no disturbance rude
8 Do they occasion; 'tis a pleasing chime.
So the unnumber'd sounds that evening store;
    The songs of birds—the whisp'ring of the leaves—
    The voice of waters—the great bell that heaves
12 With solemn sound,—and thousand others more,
    That distance of recognizance bereaves,
Make pleasing music, and not wild uproar.

No. 17. Written in October 1816. As Cowden Clarke retells the event, all night he and Keats poured over a newly acquired edition of Homer, a translation by Chapman rather than the then standard one by Pope. They recited Homer to one another until dawn when, in parting, Keats promised a new poem by ten o'clock. Keats walked two miles home, wrote the sonnet, and returned mid-morning with a near-perfect draft. Later, Clarke reports that when he read the passage of the shipwreck of Ulysses and its line "the sea had soak'd his heart through," he received from Keats "the reward of one of his delighted stares."

First published in the *Examiner* on December 1, 1816. Included in *Poems* (1817).

4 *bards:* poets
fealty: loyalty
Apollo: god of the sun, poetry, prophecy, and music
6 *demesne:* a realm or domain; also an estate
10 *ken:* scope, understanding
11–14 *stout Cortez . . . :* While Keats's detail of history passed his contemporaries without comment, Tennyson issued the correction that in fact Balboa was the first European to discover the Pacific Ocean. Cortez, the conquistador who conquered the Aztec empire, arrived later.
14 *Darien:* the Isthmus of Panama

On First Looking into Chapman's Homer

Much have I travell'd in the realms of gold,
    And many goodly states and kingdoms seen;
    Round many western islands have I been
4 Which bards in fealty to Apollo hold.
Oft of one wide expanse had I been told
    That deep-brow'd Homer ruled as his demesne;
    Yet did I never breathe its pure serene
8 Till I heard Chapman speak out loud and bold:
Then felt I like some watcher of the skies
    When a new planet swims into his ken;
Or like stout Cortez when with eagle eyes
12 He star'd at the Pacific—and all his men
Look'd at each other with a wild surmise—
    Silent, upon a peak in Darien.

No. 18. Written in October or November 1816. Cowden Clarke recalls introducing Keats to the poet Leigh Hunt and how "Keats was suddenly made a familiar of the [Hunt] household, and was always welcomed." Soon, Keats began sleeping on the sofa of the library in Hunt's "little cottage" and shortly thereafter produced this sonnet, which Clarke believed was "a characteristic appreciation of the spirit in which he had been received."

First published in *Poems* (1817).

12 *Lycid:* Lycidas, a warrior drowned violently at sea, and the central figure of Milton's elegy *Lycidas* (1638), which laments his friend Edward King, who was drowned in the Irish Sea, "dead ere his prime." (In *Adonais* [1821], Shelley's pastoral elegy to Keats, the poet-shepherd calls on all of nature to mourn with him the "Lost Angel of a ruined Paradise!")

13 *Laura:* subject of Petrarch's love poems (see next entry), believed to be Laura de Noves (d. 1348)

14 *Petrarch:* Italian poet Francesco Petrarca (1304–74), whose octave-sestet form established the Italian, or Petrarchan, sonnet

crown'd: In 1341, Petrarch was crowned laureate at Rome.

Keen, fitful gusts are whisp'ring here and there

Keen, fitful gusts are whisp'ring here and there
    Among the bushes half leafless, and dry;
    The stars look very cold about the sky,
4 And I have many miles on foot to fare.
Yet feel I little of the cool bleak air,
    Or of the dead leaves rustling drearily,
    Or of those silver lamps that burn on high,
8 Or of the distance from home's pleasant lair:
For I am brimfull of the friendliness
    That in a little cottage I have found;
Of fair-hair'd Milton's eloquent distress,
12   And all his love for gentle Lycid drown'd;
Of lovely Laura in her light green dress,
    And faithful Petrarch gloriously crown'd.

No. 19. Written in October or November 1816, shortly after the previous sonnet. The friends left are those whose company Keats had been enjoying at Hunt's cottage—his first taste of the camaraderie of poets.

First published in *Poems* (1817).

5 *atween:* between
6–7 *pearly car . . . diamond jar:* luxuries of heaven
13 *contending:* confronting or withstanding

On Leaving Some Friends at an Early Hour

Give me a golden pen, and let me lean
On heap'd up flowers, in regions clear, and far;
Bring me a tablet whiter than a star,
4 Or hand of hymning angel, when 'tis seen
The silver strings of heavenly harp atween:
And let there glide by many a pearly car,
Pink robes, and wavy hair, and diamond jar,
8 And half discovered wings, and glances keen.
The while let music wander round my ears,
And as it reaches each delicious ending,
Let me write down a line of glorious tone,
12 And full of many wonders of the spheres:
For what a height my spirit is contending!
'Tis not content so soon to be alone.

No. 20. Written (and inscribed with the date) on November 18, 1816, Tom Keats's seventeenth birthday. Keats had kept in close correspondence with his two younger brothers, and at this time, the three were living together. Tom (b. 1799) died of tuberculosis in 1818; George (b. 1797) lived until 1841.

First published in *Poems* (1817).

3 *household gods:* those minor deities who watch over house, family, and all elements of the home

5 *poles:* the North and South Poles, i.e., the far extents

7 *voluble:* effusive, engaging

8 *aye:* always

condoles: expresses sympathy for; eases

14 *shall bid our spirits fly:* Tom had already begun to show signs of his illness.

To My Brothers

Small, busy flames play through the fresh laid coals,
    And their faint cracklings o'er our silence creep
    Like whispers of the household gods that keep
4 A gentle empire o'er fraternal souls.
And while, for rhymes, I search around the poles,
    Your eyes are fix'd, as in poetic sleep,
    Upon the lore so voluble and deep,
8 That aye at fall of night our care condoles.
This is your birth-day, Tom, and I rejoice
    That thus it passes smoothly, quietly.
Many such eves of gently whisp'ring noise
12 May we together pass, and calmly try
What are this world's true joys,—ere the great voice,
    From its fair face, shall bid our spirits fly.

November 18, 1816

No. 21. Written in 1816. Keats first met the painter Benjamin Robert Haydon (1786–1846) while visiting at Hunt's cottage. Haydon was a painter of grandiose historical and religious subjects including *Christ's Triumphant Entry into Jerusalem,* for which Keats, Wordsworth (1770–1850), and fellow writers Charles Lamb (1775–1835) and William Hazlitt (1778–1830) modeled. In preparation for the painting, Haydon cast a regal life mask of Keats in 1818.

First published in *Poems* (1817).

4 *noisome:* unwholesome, noxious

6 *"singleness of aim":* among the virtues Wordsworth describes in his "Character of a Happy Warrior"

7 *hooded shame:* as a face covered in disgrace

8 *money mong'ring:* unreputable commercial exchange, the work of a huckster

9–10 *the cause . . . toiling gallantly:* Haydon was a champion of the Elgin Marbles, arguing for their acquisition by the British Museum.

14 *his country's eye:* Haydon was motivated by a strong sense of patriotism.

Addressed to Haydon

Highmindedness, a jealousy for good,
    A loving-kindness for the great man's fame,
    Dwells here and there with people of no name,
4 In noisome alley, and in pathless wood:
And where we think the truth least understood,
    Oft may be found a "singleness of aim,"
    That ought to frighten into hooded shame
8 A money mong'ring, pitiable brood.
How glorious this affection for the cause
    Of stedfast genius, toiling gallantly!
What when a stout unbending champion awes
12 Envy, and Malice to their native sty?
Unnumber'd souls breathe out a still applause,
    Proud to behold him in his country's eye.

No. 22. Written on November 20, 1816, and included in a letter Keats sent to Haydon. "Last Evening wrought me up, and I cannot forbear sending you the following," writes Keats in response to the thrill of a night of artistic conversation at Hunt's where Haydon sketched a portrait of him. In his reply, Haydon suggested shortening the penultimate line (from "Of mighty Workings in a distant Mart?"), and he also offered to send the sonnet on to Wordsworth. Keats accepted the revision and was shocked and honored at the thought of the poem's potential recipient: "The Idea of your sending it to Wordsworth put me out of breath—you know with what Reverence—I would send my Wellwishes to him." Wordsworth ultimately responded to Haydon: "The sonnet appears to be of good promise, of course neither you nor I being so highly complimented in the composition can be deemed judges altogether impartial—but it is assuredly vigorously conceived and well expressed."

First published in *Poems* (1817).

1 *Great spirits:* Wordsworth ("He" of lines 2–4), Hunt ("He" of lines 5–6), and Haydon (lines 7–8)

2 *the cloud, the cataract, the lake:* the picturesque and rugged Lake District of northern England where Wordsworth and the other Lake Poets (Coleridge and Robert Southey [1774–1843]) lived

3 *Helvellyn:* a mountain in the Lake District

5 *the rose, the violet, the spring:* Hunt favored verse that was light, passionate, and aimed "to restore the same love of Nature, and of *thinking* instead of *talking*." Due to its simplicity, some critics derided this verse as part of the "Cockney School of Poetry."

7 *stedfastness:* Haydon was adamant in his ideals, including his advocacy for the Elgin Marbles.

8 *Raphael:* In the Bible and *Paradise Lost,* the archangel Raphael tells Adam and Eve the story of creation and cautions them about the consequences of their disobedience.

14 *dumb:* silent

Addressed to the Same

Great spirits now on earth are sojourning;
He of the cloud, the cataract, the lake,
Who on Helvellyn's summit, wide awake,
4 Catches his freshness from archangel's wing:
He of the rose, the violet, the spring,
The social smile, the chain for freedom's sake:
And lo!—whose stedfastness would never take
8 A meaner sound than Raphael's whispering.
And other spirits there are standing apart
Upon the forehead of the age to come;
These, these will give the world another heart,
12 And other pulses. Hear ye not the hum
Of mighty workings?——
Listen awhile ye nations, and be dumb.

No. 23. Written in December 1816. According to a manuscript note by Woodhouse, Keats composed the sonnet on behalf of his brother George who intended it for Georgiana Augusta Wylie, the woman he would later marry.

First published in *Poems* (1817).

8 *mazy:* labyrinthine

11 *wert:* were

13 *Grace:* The three Graces, goddesses of joy, charm, and beauty, sang to the gods on Mt. Olympus and danced to the music Apollo played on his lyre.

14 *trips:* steps or treads lightly, frolics

To G.A.W.

Nymph of the downward smile, and sidelong glance,
    In what diviner moments of the day
    Art thou most lovely? When gone far astray
4 Into the labyrinths of sweet utterance?
Or when serenely wand'ring in a trance
    Of sober thought? Or when starting away,
    With careless robe, to meet the morning ray,
8 Thou spar'st the flowers in thy mazy dance?
Haply 'tis when thy ruby lips part sweetly,
    And so remain, because thou listenest:
But thou to please wert nurtured so completely
12 That I can never tell what mood is best.
I shall as soon pronounce which Grace more neatly
    Trips it before Apollo than the rest.

No. 24. Written in December 1816. Polish General Tadeusz Kosciusko (1746–1817) aided the colonists in the American Revolution before returning to fight for the liberation of his native country from Russian rule. Living in France at the end of his life, he refused to assist Napoleon because the French general would not free Poland.

First published in the *Examiner* on February 16, 1817. Included in *Poems* (1817).

3 *pealing:* ringing (as of a chorus of bells)

4 *everlasting tone:* A "favorite Speculation" of Keats was that "we shall enjoy ourselves here after by having what we called happiness on Earth repeated in a finer tone."

11 *Alfred:* Alfred the Great (849–99), King of Wessex, resisted the Danish invasion of England and instituted important English military, political, and educational reforms.

To Kosciusko

Good Kosciusko, thy great name alone
    Is a full harvest whence to reap high feeling;
    It comes upon us like the glorious pealing
4 Of the wide spheres—an everlasting tone.
And now it tells me, that in worlds unknown,
    The names of heroes, burst from clouds concealing,
    Are changed to harmonies, for ever stealing
8 Through cloudless blue, and round each silver throne.
It tells me too, that on a happy day,
    When some good spirit walks upon the earth,
        Thy name with Alfred's and the great of yore
12 Gently commingling, gives tremendous birth
To a loud hymn, that sounds far, far away
        To where the great God lives for evermore.

No. 25. Written on December 22, 1816. Tom Keats noted on the manuscript, "Written in 15 minutes." Shelley began to visit Hunt in December 1816, and there Keats likely encountered Shelley's renowned skepticism, which included questioning the practice of Christianity. In his *A Defence of Poetry*, Shelley asserts that "founders of religions" are motivated by a "celebrity" which comes via the "flattery of the gross opinions of the vulgar."

First published in *The Poetical Works of John Keats* (1876).

7 *fireside joys:* e.g., at Hunt's cottage

Lydian airs: a mode of Greek melody (to accompany poetry) which is comparative to the modern minor scale and thus soft and plaintive

8 *those with glory crown'd:* the great poets, crowned with laurel wreaths

14 *stamp:* impression, official mark, characteristic

Written in Disgust of Vulgar Superstition

The church bells toll a melancholy round,
    Calling the people to some other prayers,
    Some other gloominess, more dreadful cares,
4 More heark'ning to the sermon's horrid sound.
Surely the mind of man is closely bound
    In some black spell; seeing that each one tears
    Himself from fireside joys, and Lydian airs,
8 And converse high of those with glory crown'd.
Still, still they toll, and I should feel a damp,
    A chill as from a tomb, did I not know
That they are dying like an outburnt lamp;
12 That 'tis their sighing, wailing ere they go
    Into oblivion;—that fresh flowers will grow,
And many glories of immortal stamp.

No. 26. Written on December 30, 1816 (and inscribed with the date). The poem was Keats's answer to the challenge of a sonnet contest by Hunt on that evening. According to Cowden Clarke's firsthand account, "Keats won as to time," and as he recited the poem for the first time, Hunt responded to lines 10 and 11: "Ah! that's perfect! Bravo Keats!"

First published in *Poems* (1817). Keats's and Hunt's identically titled sonnets were published side-by-side in the *Examiner* on September 21, 1817, and in the *Monthly Repository* in October 1817.

4 *mead:* meadow

On the Grasshopper and Cricket

The poetry of earth is never dead:
    When all the birds are faint with the hot sun,
    And hide in cooling trees, a voice will run
4 From hedge to hedge about the new-mown mead;
That is the Grasshopper's—he takes the lead
    In summer luxury,—he has never done
    With his delights; for when tired out with fun
8 He rests at ease beneath some pleasant weed.
The poetry of earth is ceasing never:
    On a lone winter evening, when the frost
        Has wrought a silence, from the stove there shrills
12 The Cricket's song, in warmth increasing ever,
    And seems to one in drowsiness half lost,
        The Grasshopper's among some grassy hills.

December 30, 1816

No. 27. Written on January 31, 1817.
First published in the *Examiner* on February 23, 1817.

1 *vapours:* clouds, fog
3 *gentle south:* the warm southern wind
5 *anxious month:* i.e., January
11 *sheaves:* a bundle of cut grain or bound pieces of paper
12 *Sappho:* Greek poet (fl. c. 600 B.C.) known only through fragments of her love poems

After dark vapours have oppressed our plains

After dark vapours have oppressed our plains
For a long dreary season, comes a day
Born of the gentle south, and clears away
4 From the sick heavens all unseemly stains.
The anxious month, relieving from its pains,
Takes as a long lost right the feel of May,
The eyelids with the passing coolness play,
8 Like rose-leaves with the drip of summer rains.
And calmest thoughts come round us—as, of leaves
Budding—fruit ripening in stillness—autumn suns
Smiling at eve upon the quiet sheaves—
12 Sweet Sappho's cheek—a sleeping infant's breath—
The gradual sand that through an hour glass runs—
A woodland rivulet—a poet's death.

No. 28. Possibly written in 1816 or 1817. The identity of the young lady is not known.

First published in *Life, Letters, and Literary Remains of John Keats* (1848).

4 *content:* comprise
bier: frame used to carry a coffin to a graveside
7 *Apollo's very leaves:* laurel leaves, a laurel wreath
12 *abject:* low, degraded
13 *mailed:* armored, as with chain mail

To a Young Lady Who Sent Me a Laurel Crown

Fresh morning gusts have blown away all fear
    From my glad bosom—now from gloominess
    I mount for ever—not an atom less
4 Than the proud laurel shall content my bier.
No! by the eternal stars! or why sit here
    In the sun's eye, and 'gainst my temples press
    Apollo's very leaves—woven to bless
8 By thy white fingers, and thy spirit clear.
Lo! who dares say, "Do this"?—Who dares call down
    My will from its own purpose? who say, "Stand,"
Or "Go"? This very moment I would frown
12   On abject Caesars—not the stoutest band
Of mailed heroes should tear off my crown:—
    Yet would I kneel and kiss thy gentle hand!

No. 29. Written late in 1816 or early in 1817. According to Woodhouse, one evening after dinner Hunt and Keats crowned each other with laurels. Shortly thereafter, visitors arrived at the cottage, and while Hunt took off his crown, Keats kept his on with somewhat mock indignity that he should remove it for any reason. In the aftermath of the event, Keats was troubled by his prideful actions and wrote to his friend Benjamin Bailey in a letter, "I hope Apollo is [not] angered at my having made a Mockery at him at Hunt's."

First published in *The Times* (London) on May 18, 1914.

1 *Minutes are flying swiftly:* The phrase seems to indicate that this poem is the product of another sonnet contest with Hunt.

3 *delphic:* oracular, as from the oracle at Delphi

fain: happily

6 *ambitious:* Keats is in the midst of writing his four-thousand-line epic, *Endymion,* "a test, a trial of my Powers of Imagination," which will take him "but a dozen paces towards the Temple of Fame."

8 *coronet:* crown (i.e., the laurel wreath)

9 *dream:* Keats: "The Imagination may be compared to Adam's dream—he awoke and found it truth." In *Paradise Lost,* Adam dreams Eve's creation out of his own rib, and when he awakes, she is beside him.

On Receiving a Laurel Crown from Leigh Hunt

Minutes are flying swiftly; and as yet
    Nothing unearthly has enticed my brain
    Into a delphic labyrinth. I would fain
4 Catch an immortal thought to pay the debt
I owe to the kind poet who has set
    Upon my ambitious head a glorious gain—
    Two bending laurel sprigs—'tis nearly pain
8 To be conscious of such a coronet.
Still time is fleeting, and no dream arises
    Gorgeous as I would have it—only I see
A trampling down of what the world most prizes,
12 Turbans and crowns, and blank regality;
And then I run into most wild surmises
    Of all the many glories that may be.

No. 30. Written late in 1816 or early in 1817 on the same occasion as the previous sonnet. The ladies are the visitors who arrived at Hunt's cottage.

First published in the *Times* (London) on May 18, 1914.

2 *bay tree:* laurel tree

3 *glee:* a song

7 *halcyon:* a bird (kingfisher) believed to calm the waves when it rests upon the ocean

13 *palm:* The palm leaf is carried as an ancient symbol of triumph or glory.

To the Ladies Who Saw Me Crown'd

What is there in the universal earth
More lovely than a wreath from the bay tree?
Haply a halo round the moon—a glee
4 Circling from three sweet pair of lips in mirth;
And haply you will say the dewy birth
Of morning roses—riplings tenderly
Spread by the halcyon's breast upon the sea—
8 But these comparisons are nothing worth.
Then is there nothing in the world so fair?
The silvery tears of April?—Youth of May?
Or June that breathes out life for butterflies?
12 No—none of these can from my favorite bear
Away the palm; yet shall it ever pay
Due reverence to your most sovereign eyes.

No. 31. Written in February 1817. Cowden Clarke recalls this sonnet as "another example of [Keats's] promptly suggestive imagination, and uncommon facility in giving it utterance." Keats had returned home and found Clarke "asleep on the sofa" with a copy of Chaucer open to the "pleasant tale" (*The Flower and the Leaf*). Keats's sonnet response was, according to Clarke, "an extempore effusion, and without the alteration of a single word."

First published in the *Examiner* on March 16, 1817.

1 *copse:* a dense growth, a thicket
8 *linnet:* a small finch

This pleasant tale is like a little copse

This pleasant tale is like a little copse:
The honied lines do freshly interlace,
To keep the reader in so sweet a place,
4 So that he here and there full hearted stops;
And oftentimes he feels the dewy drops
Come cool and suddenly against his face,
And by the wandering melody may trace
8 Which way the tender-legged linnet hops.
Oh! what a power has white simplicity!
What mighty power has this gentle story!
I, that do ever feel athirst for glory,
12 Could at this moment be content to lie
Meekly upon the grass, as those whose sobbings
Were heard of none beside the mournful robbins.

No. 32. Written in February 1817. Cowden Clarke recounts the evening on which Keats received the final proofs for his first collection, *Poems*, along with a request for a dedication "forthwith." Keats "withdrew to a side-table, and in the buzz of a mixed conversation (for there were several friends in the room) he composed and brought to Charles Ollier, the publisher, the Dedication Sonnet to Leigh Hunt." The poem was, according to Clarke, "an extraordinary performance: added to which the non-alteration of a single word in the poem (a circumstance that was noted at the time) claims for it a merit with rare parallel."

First published in *Poems* (1817) as the "Dedication."

3 *wreathed incense:* as with an ancient offering to the gods

5 *nymph:* a female spirit or daemon who inhabits and governs a specific place or natural element

6–7 *ears of corn . . . violets:* offerings

8 *Flora:* Roman name of the Greek god of flowers and springtime, Chloris

12 *Pan:* god of shepherds, flocks, and fertility

14 *these poor offerings:* the poems of this volume

To Leigh Hunt, Esq.

Glory and loveliness have passed away;
    For if we wander out in early morn,
    No wreathed incense do we see upborne
4 Into the east, to meet the smiling day:
No crowd of nymphs soft voic'd and young, and gay,
    In woven baskets bringing ears of corn,
    Roses, and pinks, and violets, to adorn
8 The shrine of Flora in her early May.
But there are left delights as high as these,
    And I shall ever bless my destiny,
That in a time, when under pleasant trees
12 Pan is no longer sought, I feel a free,
A leafy luxury, seeing I could please
    With these poor offerings, a man like thee.

No. 33. Written on March 1 or 2, 1817. Keats had been taken by Haydon to view the Elgin Marbles, ancient sculptures and friezes that were brought from Athens by Lord Elgin and installed at the British Museum. Immediately after witnessing the exhibition, Keats composed this sonnet (and the following one) and sent them to Haydon. In response to these "two noble sonnets," Haydon exclaims, "*I* know not a finer image than the comparison of a Poet unable to express his high feelings to a sick eagle looking at the Sky! . . . You filled me with fury for an hour, and with admiration for ever."

First published (with the following sonnet) in the *Examiner* and in the *Champion* on March 9, 1817.

3 *steep:* a precipitous slope
11 *these wonders:* the Elgin Marbles

On Seeing the Elgin Marbles

My spirit is too weak—mortality
    Weighs heavily on me like unwilling sleep,
    And each imagined pinnacle and steep
4 Of godlike hardship tells me I must die
Like a sick eagle looking at the sky.
    Yet 'tis a gentle luxury to weep
    That I have not the cloudy winds to keep
8 Fresh for the opening of the morning's eye.
Such dim-conceived glories of the brain
    Bring round the heart an undescribable feud;
So do these wonders a most dizzy pain,
12   That mingles Grecian grandeur with the rude
Wasting of old time—with a billowy main—
    A sun—a shadow of a magnitude.

No. 34. Written on March 1 or 2, 1817.

First published (with the previous sonnet) in the *Examiner* and in the *Champion* on March 9, 1817.

2 *these mighty things:* the Elgin Marbles

6 *rolling out:* effacing, razing
upfollow'd: subsequent
thunderings: bold poetic assertions

7 *Heliconian springs:* Mt. Helicon was the home of Apollo and the Muses, where oracular springs pour forth song.

8 *freak:* an aberration or whim

9 *numbers:* the Marbles

10 *vesture:* a vestment or garment, often a religious robe

12 *o'erweening:* arrogant, overbearing
phlegm: apathetic or ignorant self-assurance

13 *Hesperean:* occidental or Western; Hesperus, the evening star, appears in the west.

To Haydon with a Sonnet Written on Seeing the Elgin Marbles

Forgive me, Haydon, that I cannot speak
    Definitively on these mighty things;
    Forgive me that I have not eagle's wings—
4 That what I want I know not where to seek:
And think that I would not be overmeek
    In rolling out upfollow'd thunderings,
    Even to the steep of Heliconian springs,
8 Were I of ample strength for such a freak.
Think too that all those numbers should be thine;
    Whose else? In this who touch thy vesture's hem?
For when men star'd at what was most divine
12   With browless idiotism—o'erweening phlegm—
Thou hadst beheld the Hesperean shine
    Of their star in the east and gone to worship them.

No. 35. Probably written in March 1817. The subject of the poem is a contemporary "gem," a glass reproduction of a cameo, here depicting the mythical figure of Leander drowning while swimming the Hellespont. A manuscript note from Woodhouse reports that "I believe it was once Keats's intention to write a series of Sonnets & short poems on Some of Tassie's [the reproduction artist's] gems." Keats wrote this sonnet for Jane Reynolds, older sister of his close friend John Reynolds, at a time when he often visited the Reynolds's house.

First published in *The Gem* in 1829.

2 *Down-looking:* Each night, Hero set a light and waited for Leander from the height of a watchtower.

5 *could not see:* From the tower on her side of the strait, Hero does not discover Leander's fate until his body washes up on shore.

9 *toiling:* The current through the strait is intense, and the youthful Leander struggles through it before finally losing his strength.

10 *swooning:* losing consciousness

On a Leander Which Miss Reynolds, My Kind Friend, Gave Me

Come hither all sweet maidens, soberly
    Down-looking—aye, and with a chastened light
    Hid in the fringes of your eyelids white—
4 And meekly let your fair hands joined be.
So gentle are ye that ye could not see,
    Untouch'd, a victim of your beauty bright—
    Sinking away to his young spirit's night,
8 Sinking bewilder'd mid the dreary sea:
'Tis young Leander toiling to his death.
    Nigh swooning, he doth purse his weary lips
        For Hero's cheek and smiles against her smile.
12 O horrid dream—see how his body dips
        Dead heavy—arms and shoulders gleam awhile:
He's gone—up bubbles all his amorous breath.

No. 36. Written in March 1817. Hunt's long poem, *The Story of Rimini,* re-tells the story of Dante's lovers Paolo and Francesca in a style that uses the looser rhyme and open vernacular associated with the so-called Cockney School of which the young Keats was said to be a member. A new edition of *Rimini* had been published in February 1817.

First published in *Life, Letters, and Literary Remains of John Keats* (1848).

6 *Hesperus:* the evening, or western, star
7 *numbers:* poetic measures, verses
8 *her hunting:* Diana, the huntress, is also the moon-goddess.
14 *sere:* withered, pale

On 'The Story of Rimini'

Who loves to peer up at the morning sun,
    With half-shut eyes and comfortable cheek,
    Let him with this sweet tale full often seek
4 For meadows where the little rivers run.
Who loves to linger with that brightest one
    Of heaven, Hesperus—let him lowly speak
    These numbers to the night and starlight meek,
8 Or moon, if that her hunting be begun.
He who knows these delights, and, too, is prone
    To moralize upon a smile or tear,
Will find at once a region of his own,
12   A bower for his spirit, and will steer
To alleys where the fir-tree drops its cone,
    Where robins hop, and fallen leaves are sere.

No. 37. Written on April 17, 1817. Keats had gone "into the country" to "be alone to improve" himself and to set upon the task of writing his *Endymion,* which he believed would be "a trial of my Powers of Imagination." This sonnet was written on the Isle of Wight and included in a letter to Reynolds in which Keats confessed, "I have been rather *narvus*—and the passage in Lear—'Do you not hear the Sea?'—has haunted me intensely." In *King Lear,* Edgar leads his blind father, the Earl of Gloucester, through the heath near Dover and asks, "Hark, do you hear the sea?" His father replies, "No, truly" (IV.vi.4–5).

First published in the *Champion* on August 17, 1817.

3 *gluts:* satiates, floods

4 *Hecate:* The cousin of the huntress Diana, Hecate, the "distant one," is associated with mysteries of witchcraft and the moon, and hence the tides.

9 *vext:* vexed

11 *dinned:* overcome with oppressive noise

14 *start:* startle

quired: choired, i.e., sang in unison

On the Sea

It keeps eternal whisperings around
Desolate shores, and with its mighty swell
Gluts twice ten thousand caverns; till the spell
4 Of Hecate leaves them their old shadowy sound.
Often 'tis in such gentle temper found
That scarcely will the very smallest shell
Be moved for days from whence it sometime fell,
8 When last the winds of heaven were unbound.
O ye who have your eyeballs vext and tir'd,
Feast them upon the wideness of the sea;
O ye whose ears are dinned with uproar rude,
12 Or fed too much with cloying melody—
Sit ye near some old cavern's mouth and brood
Until ye start, as if the sea nymphs quired.

No. 38. Probably written in 1817. In the story of Nebuchadnezzar told in the book of Daniel (chs. 2–4), the rancorous king complains, "I have dreamed a dream, and my spirit was troubled to know the dream." He demands, under penalty of dismemberment, that his wise men "shew me the dream, and the interpretation thereof," but he refuses to reveal any part of the dream itself. When all of his magicians, astrologers, and sorcerers plead that "there is none other that can shew it before the king, except the gods," the king orders all the wise men of Babylon destroyed. Daniel, hearing this fate, prays to God for help and one night is delivered the king's "terrible" vision of a creature with a head of gold and other parts of silver, brass, iron, and clay. Daniel interprets this as a composite image of the kingdoms of Babylon, and to Nebuchadnezzar he declares, "Thou art this head of gold," the greatest at the top. In response, the king constructs a massive "image of gold" which he commands his subjects to worship.

First published in *Literary Anecdotes of the Nineteenth Century,* vol. II (1896).

1 *live with owls and bats:* In a later dream, Nebuchadnezzar is a tree that a "holy one from heaven" decrees be cut down because its "kingdom is departed." Following Daniel's interpretation, the king allows himself to be "driven from men" into the wilderness until "his hairs were grown like eagles' *feathers,* and his nails like birds' *claws.*" At the end of this trial, Nebuchadnezzar lifts up his eyes and knows that, indeed, "the heavens do rule."

4 *naumachia:* a mock naval battle

5 *"good king of cats":* In *Romeo and Juliet,* Mercutio taunts Tybalt with this moniker, threatening to take all of his nine lives (III.i.77).

11 *loggerheads:* thick-headed people, fools
chapmen: peddlers

12 *sot:* a drunk, a fool

14 *"Ye are that head of gold":* Daniel 2:38

Before he went to live with owls and bats

Before he went to live with owls and bats,
  Nebuchadnezzar had an ugly dream,
  Worse than a housewife's, when she thinks her cream
4 Made a naumachia for mice and rats:
So scared, he sent for that "good king of cats,"
  Young Daniel, who did straightway pluck the beam
  From out his eye, and said—"I do not deem
8 Your sceptre worth a straw, your cushions old door mats."
A horrid nightmare, similar somewhat,
  Of late has haunted a most valiant crew
    Of loggerheads and chapmen;—we are told
12 That any Daniel, though he be a sot,
  Can make their lying lips turn pale of hue,
    By drawling out—"Ye are that head of gold!"

No. 39. Written on January 16, 1818. Mrs. Reynolds was the mother of Keats's good friend John Reynolds and his four sisters, Jane, Mariane, Eliza, and Charlotte.

First published in *The Comic Annual* (1830).

1 *climacteric:* a critical age in life
4 *segments:* the slitted eyes of a cat
13 *lists:* field for jousting

To Mrs. Reynolds's Cat

Cat! who hast past thy grand climacteric,
    How many mice and rats hast in thy days
    Destroy'd?—how many tit bits stolen? Gaze
4 With those bright languid segments green and prick
Those velvet ears—but prythee do not stick
    Thy latent talons in me—and upraise
    Thy gentle mew—and tell me all thy frays
8 Of fish and mice and rats and tender chick.
Nay, look not down, nor lick thy dainty wrists—
    For all the wheezy asthma—and for all
Thy tail's tip is nicked off—and though the fists
12   Of many a maid have given thee many a maul,
Still is that fur as soft as when the lists
    In youth thou enter'dst on glass bottled wall.

No. 40. Written on January 22, 1818. Writing to his friend Bailey, Keats tells of re-reading the *Tragedy of King Lear* and how he "felt the greatness of the thing up to the writing of a Sonnet preparatory thereto." Later, in a letter to his brothers, he offers the sonnet as evidence for "a little change [that] has taken place in my intellect lately—I cannot bear to be uninterested or unemployed, I, who for so long a time, have been addicted to passiveness."

First published in the *Plymouth and Devonport Weekly Journal* on November 8, 1838.

1 *serene:* clear, brilliant, tranquil

2 *syren:* siren, a fantastic, female-bird creature whose enchanting song lures sailors off course and to their deaths

queen of far-away: Hecate is the goddess of the "far-away" and the mysterious.

6 *impassion'd:* animated

7 *assay:* examine, assess

8 *this Shaksperean fruit:* the play *King Lear*

9 *Albion:* the Celtic name for England

14 *phoenix:* A bird that lives for five hundred years, then erupts into flames and is consumed, and finally resurrects itself from its ashes.

On Sitting Down to Read 'King Lear' Once Again

O golden-tongued Romance, with serene lute!
    Fair plumed syren, queen of far-away!
    Leave melodizing on this wintry day,
4 Shut up thine olden pages, and be mute.
Adieu! for, once again, the fierce dispute
    Betwixt damnation and impassion'd clay
    Must I burn through; once more humbly assay
8 The bitter-sweet of this Shaksperean fruit.
Chief Poet! and ye clouds of Albion,
    Begetters of our deep eternal theme!
When through the old oak forest I am gone,
12 Let me not wander in a barren dream:
But, when I am consumed in the fire,
Give me new phoenix wings to fly at my desire.

No. 41. Written in January 1818. In a letter to John Reynolds on January 31, 1818, Keats cycles through prose, song, and the verse epistle of a "serious poetical Letter" before admitting "I cannot write sense this Morning—however you shall have some—I will copy my last Sonnet."

First published in *Life, Letters, and Literary Remains of John Keats* (1848).

2 *glean'd:* collected the fragments, assembled the grain felled by a reaper

3 *charactry:* charactery, i.e., a system of symbols or characters

4 *garners:* granaries

6 *high romance:* a poem of chivalric quest such as *Endymion*, on which Keats was then working

14 *fame:* In a letter to Benjamin Bailey on October 8, 1817, Keats quotes an earlier response to his brother George: "As to what you say about my being a Poet, I can retu[r]n no answer but by saying that the high Idea I have of poetical fame makes me think I see it towering to[o] high above me. At any rate I have no right to talk until Endymion is finished." Keats completed *Endymion* in late November 1817.

When I have fears that I may cease to be

When I have fears that I may cease to be
    Before my pen has glean'd my teeming brain,
Before high piled books, in charactry,
4   Hold like rich garners the full ripen'd grain;
When I behold, upon the night's starr'd face,
    Huge cloudy symbols of a high romance,
And think that I may never live to trace
8   Their shadows, with the magic hand of chance;
And when I feel, fair creature of an hour,
    That I shall never look upon thee more,
Never have relish in the fairy power
12   Of unreflecting love;—then on the shore
Of the wide world I stand alone, and think
Till love and fame to nothingness do sink.

No. 42. Written on February 4, 1818. In his transcript notes, Woodhouse claims the addressee and inspiration of this sonnet (as well as "When I have fears") was a particular woman, although he says that she was seen by Keats "for some few moments at Vauxhall" and elsewhere merely that "Keats mentioned the circumstance of obtaining a casual sight of her."

First published in *Hood's Magazine* in September 1844.

7 *dye:* color

Time's sea hath been five years at its slow ebb

Time's sea hath been five years at its slow ebb;
    Long hours have to and fro let creep the sand,
Since I was tangled in thy beauty's web,
4   And snared by the ungloving of thy hand:
And yet I never look on midnight sky,
    But I behold thine eyes' well-memoried light;
I cannot look upon the rose's dye,
8   But to thy cheek my soul doth take its flight:
I cannot look on any budding flower,
    But my fond ear, in fancy at thy lips,
And hearkening for a love-sound, doth devour
12   Its sweets in the wrong sense.—Thou dost eclipse
Every delight with sweet remembering,
And grief unto my darling joys dost bring.

No. 43. Written on February 4, 1818. This sonnet, according to Woodhouse's transcript notes, was Keats's entry into another fifteen-minute sonnet-writing contest with Hunt and Shelley at Hunt's house. Keats, along with Shelley, was "ready within the time."

First published in the *Plymouth and Devonport Weekly Journal* on July 19, 1838.

5 *swart:* dark-skinned, exotic
8 *'twixt:* betwixt, between
Decan: the Deccan plateau in south central India
13 *green isles:* the Nile meets the Mediterranean in an expansive delta

To the Nile

Son of the old moon-mountains African!
    Chief of the pyramid and crocodile!
    We call thee fruitful, and, that very while,
4 A desert fills our seeing's inward span;
Nurse of swart nations since the world began,
    Art thou so fruitful? or dost thou beguile
    Such men to honor thee, who, worn with toil,
8 Rest for a space 'twixt Cairo and Decan?
O may dark fancies err! they surely do;
    'Tis ignorance that makes a barren waste
Of all beyond itself: thou dost bedew
12   Green rushes like our rivers, and dost taste
The pleasant sun-rise; green isles hast thou too,
    And to the sea as happily dost haste.

No. 44. Written on February 5, 1818.

First published in *Life, Letters, and Literary Remains of John Keats* (1848).

5 *Elfin-Poet:* Spenser, the author of the fantastic world of *The Faerie Queen*

7 *Phoebus:* the god Apollo

quell: a bow, such as Apollo, the god of archery, might carry

8 *fire-wing'd:* Apollo drove the sun-chariot across the sky each day.

Spenser, a jealous honorer of thine

Spenser, a jealous honorer of thine,
    A forester deep in thy midmost trees,
Did last eve ask my promise to refine
4   Some English that might strive thine ear to please.
But Elfin-Poet, 'tis impossible
    For an inhabitant of wintry earth
To rise like Phoebus with a golden quell,
8   Fire-wing'd, and make a morning in his mirth:
It is impossible to escape from toil
    O' the sudden, and receive thy spiriting:—
The flower must drink the nature of the soil
12   Before it can put forth its blossoming.
Be with me in the summer days, and I
Will for thine honor and his pleasure try.

No. 45. Written on February 8, 1818. According to Stillinger, this sonnet replies to the final lines of a sonnet written by Reynolds: "dark eyes are dearer far / Than those that mock the hyacinthine-bell."

First published in *Life, Letters, and Literary Remains of John Keats* (1848).

2 *Cynthia:* the Virgin Moon. She enchants the shepherd-hero of Keats's long poem *Endymion.*

3 *Hesperus:* the evening star which, appearing in the west, marks the occidental or Western world

4 *bosomer:* one who embraces

Blue!—'Tis the life of heaven—the domain

Blue!—'Tis the life of heaven—the domain
    Of Cynthia:—the wide palace of the sun;
The tent of Hesperus and all his train;
4   The bosomer of clouds gold, grey, and dun.
Blue!—'Tis the life of waters—Ocean,
    And all its vassal streams, pools numberless,
May rage, and foam, and fret, but never can
8   Subside, if not to dark blue nativeness.
Blue!—gentle cousin to the forest green,
    Married to green in all the sweetest flowers—
Forget-me-not—the blue-bell—and, that queen
12   Of secrecy, the violet:—What strange powers
Hast thou, as a mere shadow?—But how great,
When in an eye thou art, alive with fate!

No. 46. Written on February 19, 1818. Writing to John Reynolds that morning, Keats considers "an old Comparison for our urging on—the Bee hive," but adds, "however it seems to me that we should rather be the flower than the Bee—for it is a false notion that more is gained by receiving than giving—no the receiver and the giver are equal in their benefits," and concludes, "let us not therefore go hurrying about and collecting honey-bee like, buzzing here and there impatiently from a knowledge of what is to be arrived at: but let us open our leaves like a flower and be passive and receptive." Keats then confesses, "I was led into these thoughts, my dear Reynolds, by the beauty of the morning operating on a sense of Idleness—I have not read any Books—the Morning said I was right—I had no Idea but of the Morning and the Thrush said I was right—seeming to say—" Here, he presents the sonnet, enclosed in quotes, as the voice of the thrush. Afterward, he demurs, "Now I am sensible all this is a mere sophistication, however it may neighbour to any truths, to excuse my own indolence."

First published in *Life, Letters, and Literary Remains of John Keats* (1848).

6 feddest: fed

O thou whose face hath felt the winter's wind

O thou whose face hath felt the winter's wind,
Whose eye has seen the snow clouds hung in mist,
And the black-elm tops 'mong the freezing stars,
4 To thee the spring will be a harvest-time.
O thou whose only book has been the light
Of supreme darkness which thou feddest on
Night after night, when Phoebus was away,
8 To thee the spring shall be a tripple morn.
O fret not after knowledge—I have none,
And yet my song comes native with the warmth;
O fret not after knowledge—I have none,
12 And yet the evening listens. He who saddens
At thought of idleness cannot be idle,
And he's awake who thinks himself asleep.

No. 47. Written in early March 1818. Including the sonnet in a March 13th letter to Benjamin Bailey, Keats proposes that the ideas of the poem "may be carried" and then clarifies, "but what I am talking of—it is an old maxim of mine and of course must be well known that eve[r]y point of thought is the centre of an intellectual world—the two uppermost thoughts in a Man's mind are the poles of his World he revolves on them and every thing is southward or northward to him through their means—We take but three steps from feathers to iron." Then, Keats issues a caveat to his thesis, "Now my dear fellow I must once for all tell you I have not one Idea of the truth of any of my speculations—I shall never be a Reasoner because I care not to be in the right, when retired from bickering and in a proper philosophical temper."

First published in Leigh Hunt's *Literary Pocket-Book* (1818), a kind of date book of blank pages, poems, and essays.

Four seasons fill the measure of the year

Four seasons fill the measure of the year;
    Four seasons are there in the mind of man.
He hath his lusty spring, when fancy clear
4   Takes in all beauty with an easy span:
He hath his summer, when luxuriously
    He chews the honied cud of fair spring thoughts,
Till, in his soul dissolv'd, they come to be
8   Part of himself. He hath his autumn ports
And havens of repose, when his tired wings
    Are folded up, and he content to look
On mists in idleness: to let fair things
12   Pass by unheeded as a threshold brook.
He hath his winter too of pale misfeature,
Or else he would forget his mortal nature.

No. 48. Possibly written in April 1818. The sonnet is addressed to a friend, James Rice. That spring in Devon, Keats and his sick brother Tom were largely confined inside by poor weather; a week-long visit by Rice invigorated the sullen indoor atmosphere.

First published in *Life, Letters, and Literary Remains of John Keats* (1848).

6 *annihilate:* annihilated
8 *dilate:* expand
9 *Ind:* India
10 *Levant:* the East
12 *pant:* a quick breath, gasp, desire

To J. R.

O that a week could be an age, and we
    Felt parting and warm meeting every week;
Then one poor year a thousand years would be,
4   The flush of welcome ever on the cheek.
So could we live long life in little space;
    So time itself would be annihilate;
So a day's journey, in oblivious haze
8   To serve our joys, would lengthen and dilate.
O to arrive each Monday morn from Ind,
    To land each Tuesday from the rich Levant,
In little time a host of joys to bind,
12   And keep our souls in one eternal pant!
This morn, my friend, and yester evening taught
Me how to harbour such a happy thought.

No. 49. Written in 1818.

First published in *Life, Letters, and Literary Remains of John Keats* (1848).

2 *Cyclades:* a circle of islands in the southern Aegean Sea
6 *Jove:* chief of the gods
7 *Neptune:* god of the sea
spumy: foamy
8 *Pan:* the man-goat god of shepherds
11 *morrow:* tomorrow
13 *befel:* befell
14 *Dian:* the goddess Diana

To Homer

Standing aloof in giant ignorance,
    Of thee I hear and of the Cyclades,
As one who sits ashore and longs perchance
4   To visit dolphin-coral in deep seas.
So wast thou blind;—but then the veil was rent,
    For Jove uncurtain'd heaven to let thee live,
And Neptune made for thee a spumy tent,
8   And Pan made sing for thee his forest-hive;
Aye on the shores of darkness there is light,
    And precipices show untrodden green,
There is a budding morrow in midnight,
12   There is a triple sight in blindness keen;
Such seeing hadst thou, as it once befel
To Dian, Queen of Earth, and Heaven, and Hell.

No. 50. Written on July 1, 1818. On a walking tour of the Lake Country and Scotland with the energetic Charles Brown, Keats came to the tomb of the famous and much-loved Scottish poet Robert Burns (1759–96). He enclosed this poem in a letter to his brother Tom, in which he admits, "This Sonnet I have written in a strange mood, half asleep. I know not how it is, the Clouds, the sky, the Houses, all seem anti Grecian & anti Charlemagnish—I will endeavour to get rid of my prejudices, & tell you fairly about the Scotch." Several days later he reports to Reynolds, "One of the pleasantest means of annulling self is approaching such a shrine as the Cottage of Burns—we need not think of his misery—that is all gone—bad luck to it . . . the Sight was as rich as possible—I had no Conception that the native place of Burns was so beautiful—the Idea I had was more desolate, his rigs of Barley seemed always to me but a few strips of Green on a cold hill—O prejudice! it was rich as Devon—I endeavour'd to drink in the Prospect, that I might spin it out to you as the silkworm makes silk from Mulberry leaves—I cannot recollect it."

First published in *Life, Letters, and Literary Remains of John Keats* (1848).

5 *paly:* pale

6 *ague:* fits of cold, chills, and fever

9 *Minos:* the king of ancient Crete who later judges souls in the Underworld

On Visiting the Tomb of Burns

The town, the churchyard, and the setting sun,
    The clouds, the trees, the rounded hills all seem,
    Though beautiful, cold—strange—as in a dream
4 I dreamed long ago. Now new begun,
The short-lived, paly summer is but won
    From winter's ague, for one hour's gleam;
    Though saphire warm, their stars do never beam;
8 All is cold beauty; pain is never done
For who has mind to relish, Minos-wise,
    The real of beauty, free from that dead hue
        Sickly imagination and sick pride
12   Cast wan upon it! Burns! with honour due
        I have oft honoured thee. Great shadow, hide
Thy face—I sin against thy native skies.

No. 51. Written on July 10, 1818. Writing to his brother Tom from Scotland while continuing the walking tour, Keats promises, "I shall endeavour that you may follow our steps in this walk—it would be uninteresting in a Book of Travels—it can not be interest[ing] but by my having gone through it." He then relays a portion of their journey: "we had a gradual ascent and got among the tops of the Mountains whence In a little time I descried in the Sea Ailsa Rock 940 feet hight—it was 15 Miles distant and seemed close upon us—The effect of ailsa with the peculiar perspective of the Sea in connection with the ground we stood on, and the misty rain then falling gave me a complete Idea of a deluge—Ailsa struck me very suddenly—really I was a little alarmed." The sonnet follows. Then, Keats disclaims, "This is the only Sonnet of any worth I have of late written—I hope you will like it." Ailsa Rock—at the mouth of the Clyde off an interior western coast of Scotland—is commonly known as Ailsa Craig.

First published in Leigh Hunt's *Literary Pocket-Book* (1818).

3 *mantled:* cloaked, hidden

6 *heave . . . dreams:* Ailsa Craig is an upthrust of igneous rock.

fathom: a measure, originally equal to the length of a man's outspread arms, now equal to six feet and used principally as a measure of depth

To Ailsa Rock

Hearken, thou craggy ocean pyramid,
    Give answer by thy voice, the sea fowls' screams!
    When were thy shoulders mantled in huge streams?
4 When from the sun was thy broad forehead hid?
How long is't since the mighty power bid
    Thee heave to airy sleep from fathom dreams—
    Sleep in the lap of thunder or sunbeams,
8 Or when grey clouds are thy cold coverlid?
Thou answer'st not, for thou art dead asleep;
    Thy life is but two dead eternities,
The last in air, the former in the deep—
12   First with the whales, last with the eagle skies;
Drown'd wast thou till an earthquake made thee steep—
    Another cannot wake thy giant size!

No. 52. Written on July 11, 1818. During their pilgrimage to the cottage of Robert Burns, Keats and Charles Brown pause inside. "We went to the Cottage and took some Whiskey," Keats reports to John Reynolds, "I wrote a sonnet for the mere sake of writing some lines under the roof." In the end, Keats withholds the poem from Reynolds, claiming, "they are so bad I cannot transcribe them," a sentiment he confirms to Tom Keats: "I was determined to write a sonnet in the Cottage—I did—but it is so bad I cannot venture it here."

First published in *Life, Letters, and Literary Remains of John Keats* (1848).

3 *budded bays:* Bays (or baize) is a thick woolen cover or upholstery (thus "budded" or buttoned).

5 *barley-bree:* barley-brew, ale

6 *pledging:* toasting, vowing

8 *Fancy:* the ability to create descriptive imagery, what Hunt calls the "lighter play of imagination"

13 *bumper:* a wine or other drinking glass filled to the brim

14 *shades:* spirits, ghosts

This mortal body of a thousand days

This mortal body of a thousand days
    Now fills, O Burns, a space in thine own room,
Where thou didst dream alone on budded bays,
4   Happy and thoughtless of thy day of doom!
My pulse is warm with thine old barley-bree,
    My head is light with pledging a great soul,
My eyes are wandering, and I cannot see,
8   Fancy is dead and drunken at its goal;
Yet can I stamp my foot upon thy floor,
    Yet can I ope thy window-sash to find
The meadow thou hast tramped o'er and o'er,—
12   Yet can I think of thee till thought is blind,—
Yet can I gulp a bumper to thy name,—
O smile among the shades, for this is fame!

No. 53. Written on July 17 or 18, 1818. Toward the end of his tour, Keats's continued awe at the landscape is contrasted with the lost appeal of another aspect of Scotland, its characteristic music. To Tom he explains, "the woods seem old enough to remember t[w]o or three changes in the Crags about them—the Lake was beautiful and there was a Band at a distance by the Castle. I must say I enjoyed t[w]o or three common tunes—but nothing could stifle the horrors of a solo on the Bag-pipe." This prejudice affects his reaction to a local production of *The Stranger,* a popular German play. The melodrama concerns an adulterous wife, Mrs. Haller, who abandons her children to follow her lover. When she returns she discovers that her children have forgotten her, and she falls into suffering and penance. "When Mrs. Haller fainted down went the Curtain and out came the Bagpipe—at the heartrending, shoemending reconciliation the Piper blew amain—I never read or saw this play before; not the Bag pipe, nor the wretched players themselves were little in comparison with it—thank heaven it has been scoffed at lately almost to a fashion."

First published in the *Athenaeum* on June 7, 1873.

1 *dainties:* delicacies, pleasurable objects

3 *ninth sphere:* In the cosmology of Dante's *Divine Comedy,* a series of concentric spheres hold the atmosphere, planets, stars, etc.; the ninth is the furthest out and coincides with the ineffable.

6 *The Stranger:* the forgotten Mrs. Haller

8 *waste:* wither, decay

14 *Mumchance:* silent, idle; also, mumming, the silent art of the masquerade

Of late two dainties were before me plac'd

Of late two dainties were before me plac'd,
    Sweet, holy, pure, sacred, and innocent,
    From the ninth sphere to me benignly sent
4 That gods might know my own particular taste.
First the soft bag-pipe mourn'd with zealous haste;
    The Stranger next with head on bosom bent
    Sigh'd; rueful again the piteous bag-pipe went;
8 Again the Stranger sighings fresh did waste.
O bag-pipe, thou didst steal my heart away;
    O Stranger, thou my nerves from pipe didst charm;
O bag-pipe, thou didst reassert thy sway;
12 Again thou Stranger gav'st me fresh alarm—
Alas! I could not choose. Ah! my poor heart,
Mumchance art thou with both obliged to part.

No. 54. Written August 2, 1818. On this date Keats and Brown "went up Ben Nevis, the highest Mountain in Great Britain," an experience which Keats reports "is almost like a fly crawling up a wainscoat." Writing a long account of the journey to Tom, Keats attempts to give his brother "an Idea of the prospect from a large Mountain top" where "after a little time the Mist cleared away but still there were large Clouds about attracted by old Ben to a certain distance so as to form as it appeard large dome curtains which kept sailing about, opening and shutting at intervals here and there and everrywhere [*sic*]; so that although we did not see one vast wide extent of prospect all round we saw something perhaps finer—these cloud-veils opening with a dissolving motion and showing us the mountainous region beneath as through a loop hole." In his *Life of John Keats,* Charles Brown recounts the moment when Keats "sat on the stones, a few feet from the edge of that fearful precipice, fifteen hundred feet perpendicular from the valley below, and wrote this sonnet."

First published in the *Plymouth and Devonport Weekly Journal* on September 6, 1838.

1 *Muse:* one of nine inspirational and instructive sister-goddesses, each representing a realm of art

Read me a lesson, Muse, and speak it loud

Read me a lesson, Muse, and speak it loud
    Upon the top of Nevis, blind in mist!
I look into the chasms, and a shroud
4   Vaprous doth hide them; just so much I wist
Mankind do know of hell: I look o'erhead,
    And there is sullen mist; even so much
Mankind can tell of heaven: mist is spread
8   Before the earth beneath me; even such,
Even so vague is man's sight of himself.
    Here are the craggy stones beneath my feet;
Thus much I know, that, a poor witless elf,
12   I tread on them; that all my eye doth meet
Is mist and crag—not only on this height,
But in the world of thought and mental might.

No. 55. Probably written on September 21, 1818. Writing to John Reynolds on the 22nd, Keats congratulates and commands his newly engaged friend: "Gorge the honey of life." Yet he soon laments his own bittersweet condition: "I pity you as much that it cannot last for ever, as I do myself now drinking bitters.—Give yourself up to it—you cannot help it—and I have a Consolation in thinking so—I never was in love—Yet the voice and the shape of a woman has haunted me these two days—at such a time when the relief, the feverous relief of Poetry seems a much less crime—This morning Poetry has conquered—I have relapsed into those abstractions which are my only life—I feel escaped from a new strange and threatening sorrow.—And I am thankful for it—There is an awful warmth about my heart like a load of Immortality." He includes this poem, "a free translation of a Sonnet of Ronsard." Pierre de Ronsard's "Nature ornant Cassandre, qui devoit" is from his *Les amours de Cassandre*. Keats explains the twelve-line form thus: "I had not the original by me when I wrote it, and did not recollect the purport of the last lines."

First published in *Life, Letters, and Literary Remains of John Keats* (1848).

1 *Cassandra:* Greek princess possessing the ability to foretell the future but doomed always to be suspected and disbelieved

2 *meet:* fitting, suitable

8 *Olympus:* mountain home of the Greek gods

Nature withheld Cassandra in the skies

Nature withheld Cassandra in the skies
    For meet adornment a full thousand years;
She took their cream of beauty, fairest dyes,
4   And shaped and tinted her above all peers.
Love meanwhile held her dearly with his wings,
    And underneath their shadow charm'd her eyes
To such a richness, that the cloudy kings
8   Of high Olympus utter'd slavish sighs.
When I beheld her on the earth descend,
    My heart began to burn—and only pains,
They were my pleasures, they my sad life's end;
12   Love pour'd her beauty into my warm veins.

No. 56. Written in March 1819. Keats places this sonnet in the midst of a long letter to his brother George and his wife which he assembled over many months and which spans feelings from confidence to despair. The sonnet follows an apologetic introduction: "I am ever affraid [*sic*] that your anxiety for me will lead you to fear for the violence of my temperament continually smothered down: for that reason I did not intend to have sent you the following sonnet—but look over the two last pages and ask yourselves whether I have not that in me which will well bear the buffets of the world. It will be the best comment on my sonnet; it will show you that it was written with no Agony but that of ignorance; with no thirst of any thing but knowledge when pushed to the point though the first steps to it were throug[h] my human passions—they went away, and I wrote with my Mind—and perhaps I must confess a little bit of my heart."

First published in *Life, Letters, and Literary Remains of John Keats* (1848).

9 *lease:* life span
12 *ensigns:* pennants, emblems of allegiance or rank
14 *meed:* reward

Why did I laugh tonight? No voice will tell

Why did I laugh tonight? No voice will tell:
    No god, no demon of severe response,
Deigns to reply from heaven or from hell.
4   Then to my human heart I turn at once—
Heart! thou and I are here sad and alone;
    Say, wherefore did I laugh? O mortal pain!
O darkness! darkness! ever must I moan,
8   To question heaven and hell and heart in vain!
Why did I laugh? I know this being's lease—
    My fancy to its utmost blisses spreads:
Yet could I on this very midnight cease,
12   And the world's gaudy ensigns see in shreds.
Verse, fame, and beauty are intense indeed,
But death intenser—death is life's high meed.

No. 57. Written in April 1819. Later in that spring's substantial letter to George and Georgiana, Keats includes this sonnet, which is, he says, the product of a Dantean dream: "The fifth canto of Dante pleases me more and more—it is that one in which he meets with Paulo and Francesca—I had passed many days in rather a low state of mind and in the midst of them I dreamt of being in that region of Hell. The dream was one of the most delightful enjoyments I ever had in my life—I floated about the whirling atmosphere as it is described with a beautiful figure to whose lips mine were joined [as] it seem'd for an age—and in the midst of all this cold and darkness I was warm—even flowery tree tops sprung up and we rested on them sometimes with the lightness of a cloud till the wind blew us away again—I tried a Sonnet upon it—there are fourteen lines but nothing of what I felt in it—o that I could dream it every night."

First published in the *Indicator* on June 28, 1820.

1 *Hermes:* the messenger of the gods and patron of travelers, merchants, and thieves. Jove, who has stolen the nymph Io only to be discovered by Juno, calls on the devious Hermes against the hundred-eyed Argus whom a jealous Juno has employed to keep watch over Io. Disguised as a shepherd, Hermes plays the flute and tells stories until all of Argus's eyes close in sleep, whereupon Hermes kills him. In another of his duties, Hermes chaperones souls to the underworld.

his feathers light: Hermes' winged feet

3 *Delphic reed:* a prophetic flute such as Apollo plays

spright: sprite, spirit

5 *dragon-world:* Hades, hell

7 *Ida:* Jove, who was raised in a cave on its slopes, is worshipped at Mount Ida on the island of Crete.

8 *Tempe:* a deep valley that is home to the river gods (among them Inachus, desperate father of the missing Io) and where Jove gained and lost his lovely nymph.

Jove: chief of the gods, husband to Juno

9 *second circle:* In Dante's *Inferno*, the second circle of hell is reserved for sins of lust. The lovers Paolo and Francesca are confined there.

As Hermes once took to his feathers light

As Hermes once took to his feathers light,
    When lulled Argus, baffled, swoon'd and slept,
So on a Delphic reed, my idle spright
4   So play'd, so charm'd, so conquer'd, so bereft
The dragon-world of all its hundred eyes;
    And, seeing it asleep, so fled away—
Not to pure Ida with its snow-cold skies,
8   Nor unto Tempe, where Jove griev'd a day,
But to that second circle of sad hell,
    Where in the gust, the whirlwind, and the flaw
Of rain and hail-stones, lovers need not tell
12   Their sorrows. Pale were the sweet lips I saw,
Pale were the lips I kiss'd, and fair the form
I floated with, about that melancholy storm.

No. 58. Written in 1819, according to Charles Brown's original dating of the manuscripts. However, the poem's significant later revision—undertaken by Keats on a page of his edition of Shakespeare while en route by ship to convalesce in Italy in late September 1820—led to the title "Keats's Last Sonnet" in early editions. (Keats died in Italy in February 1821.)

First published in the *Plymouth and Devonport Weekly Journal* on September 27, 1838.

4 *eremite:* a religious recluse, e.g., a hermit or a monk
6 *ablution:* cleansing, baptism

Bright star, would I were stedfast as thou art

Bright star, would I were stedfast as thou art—
    Not in lone splendor hung aloft the night,
And watching, with eternal lids apart,
4   Like nature's patient, sleepless eremite,
The moving waters at their priestlike task
    Of pure ablution round earth's human shores,
Or gazing on the new soft-fallen mask
8   Of snow upon the mountains and the moors;
No—yet still stedfast, still unchangeable,
    Pillow'd upon my fair love's ripening breast,
To feel for ever its soft swell and fall,
12   Awake for ever in a sweet unrest,
Still, still to hear her tender-taken breath,
And so live ever—or else swoon to death.

No. 59. Probably written in April 1819. Keats copies out this poem and the next two sonnets on fame in a letter to George Keats, saying they are among "some of my old sins—that is to say sonnets." In composing them he has "for the most part dash'd of[f] my lines in a hurry."

First published in the *Plymouth and Devonport Weekly Journal* on October 11, 1838.

3 *embower'd:* tucked safe away in a place of refuge, such as a bower

7 *poppy:* Opium is a derivative of the opium poppy.

13 *wards:* the pins of a lock cylinder, which allow only the proper key to pass

Sonnet to Sleep

O soft embalmer of the still midnight,
    Shutting with careful fingers and benign
Our gloom-pleas'd eyes, embower'd from the light,
4   Enshaded in forgetfulness divine:
O soothest Sleep! if so it please thee, close,
    In midst of this thine hymn, my willing eyes,
Or wait the Amen ere thy poppy throws
8   Around my bed its lulling charities.
Then save me or the passed day will shine
    Upon my pillow, breeding many woes:
Save me from curious conscience, that still hoards
12   Its strength for darkness, burrowing like the mole;
Turn the key deftly in the oiled wards,
    And seal the hushed casket of my soul.

No. 60. Written on April 30, 1819. The poem appears in a letter to George along with the preceding and the next sonnets.

First published in *Ladies' Companion* in August 1837.

7 *jilt:* one who attracts and then discards lovers capriciously

9 *Nilus:* the River Nile

10 *Potiphar:* Chapter 39 of Genesis tells the story of Joseph's service in the house of Potiphar, an official of the pharaoh in Egypt. Potiphar's wife flirts with Joseph incessantly. Once while trying to evade her advances, Joseph leaves his cloak behind in her hands. With the garment as evidence, she claims that Joseph has thrown himself upon her. When he hears this accusation, the jealous Potiphar imprisons Joseph.

On Fame

Fame, like a wayward girl, will still be coy
    To those who woo her with too slavish knees,
But makes surrender to some thoughtless boy,
4   And dotes the more upon a heart at ease;
She is a gipsey, will not speak to those
    Who have not learnt to be content without her;
A jilt, whose ear was never whisper'd close,
8   Who thinks they scandal her who talk about her;
A very gipsey is she, Nilus born,
    Sister-in-law to jealous Potiphar;
Ye love-sick bards, repay her scorn for scorn;
12   Ye artists lovelorn, madmen that ye are!
Make your best bow to her and bid adieu;
Then, if she likes it, she will follow you.

No. 61. Written on April 30, 1819. The poem appears in a letter of that date to George Keats along with the two preceding sonnets.

First published in *Life, Letters, and Literary Remains of John Keats* (1848).

3 *vexes:* agitates, troubles
4 *maidenhood:* virginity, purity
7 *Naiad:* a nymph, a local goddess of a stream, pool, or spring
8 *grot:* grotto
13 *teasing:* combing a material such as wool to collect fibers for spinning
14 *miscreed:* a mistaken tenet or belief

On Fame

"You cannot eat your cake and have it too." — Proverb

How fever'd is the man who cannot look
Upon his mortal days with temperate blood,
Who vexes all the leaves of his life's book,
4 And robs his fair name of its maidenhood;
It is as if the rose should pluck herself,
Or the ripe plum finger its misty bloom,
As if a Naiad, like a meddling elf,
8 Should darken her pure grot with muddy gloom;
But the rose leaves herself upon the briar,
For winds to kiss and grateful bees to feed,
And the ripe plum still wears its dim attire,
12 The undisturbed lake has crystal space;
Why then should man, teasing the world for grace,
Spoil his salvation for a fierce miscreed?

No. 62. Written in April or May 1819. This is the final poem included in the long letter Keats sends to his brother George and his wife in America in May. Before he copies the sonnet, he introduces his formal intentions: "I have been endeavouring to discover a better sonnet stanza than we have. The legitimate does not suit the language over-well from the pouncing rhymes—the other kind appears too elegaic [*sic*]—and the couplet at the end of it has seldom a pleasing effect—I do not pretend to have succeeded—it will explain itself." The "legitimate" stanza to which Keats refers is the Petrarchan sonnet, which rhymes its octave *abba abba* and then offers various sestets—*cde cde; cdcdcd;* etc.—but never a closing couplet. The "other kind" is the Shakespearean sonnet which consists of three quatrains and a closing couplet: *abab cdcd efef gg.*

First published in the *Plymouth, Devonport, and Stonehouse News* on October 15, 1836.

2 *Andromeda:* An Ethiopian princess whose mother praises her daughter's beauty beyond that of the sea nymphs. A wrathful Poseiden sends a sea serpent to destroy their city, and to appease the god, Andromeda is chained to a rock near the ocean in sacrifice. She is saved by the hero Perseus.

7 *lyre:* Apollo's stringed instrument, used to accompany sung —and thus *lyric*—poetry

9 *meet:* fit, matched

11 *Midas:* The mythic king Midas—granted one wish—asks that everything he touch turn to gold. When this includes his food and drink, he nearly starves before the wish is repealed.

12 *bay wreath crown:* a crown of laurels, symbolic of Apollo and presented to honor a poet laureate

If by dull rhymes our English must be chain'd

If by dull rhymes our English must be chain'd,
  And, like Andromeda, the sonnet sweet
    Fetter'd, in spite of pained loveliness;
4 Let us find out, if we must be constrain'd,
  Sandals more interwoven and complete
To fit the naked foot of Poesy;
    Let us inspect the lyre, and weigh the stress
8 Of every chord, and see what may be gain'd
  By ear industrious, and attention meet;
    Misers of sound and syllable, no less
Than Midas of his coinage, let us be
12 Jealous of dead leaves in the bay wreath crown;
So, if we may not let the muse be free,
  She will be bound with garlands of her own.

No. 63. Written in 1819. According to Stillinger, this poem and the next are, along with a contemporary poem of explicit address—"To Fanny"—directed to Fanny Brawne, the object of Keats's love and the recipient of many passionate letters. In a letter written to Fanny two days after a move that still kept him a distance from her, Keats closes, "O my love, your lips are growing sweet again to my fancy—I must forget them."

First published in the *Plymouth and Devonport Weekly Journal* on October 4, 1838.

10 *holinight:* a night to follow a day of pleasure or holiday

12 *woof:* In weaving, the fibers of the woof are threaded across the lines of the warp, which runs the length of the fabric.

13 *missal:* prayer book

The day is gone, and all its sweets are gone

The day is gone, and all its sweets are gone!
    Sweet voice, sweet lips, soft hand, and softer breast,
Warm breath, light whisper, tender semi-tone,
4   Bright eyes, accomplish'd shape, and lang'rous waist!
Faded the flower and all its budded charms,
    Faded the sight of beauty from my eyes,
Faded the shape of beauty from my arms,
8   Faded the voice, warmth, whiteness, paradise,
Vanish'd unseasonably at shut of eve,
    When the dusk holiday—or holinight—
Of fragrant curtain'd Love begins to weave
12   The woof of darkness, thick, for hid delight;
But, as I've read Love's missal through to-day,
He'll let me sleep, seeing I fast and pray.

No. 64. Written in 1819.

First published in *Life, Letters, and Literary Remains of John Keats* (1848).

I cry your mercy—pity—love!—aye, love

I cry your mercy—pity—love!—aye, love,
    Merciful love that tantalises not,
One-thoughted, never wand'ring, guileless love,
4   Unmask'd, and being seen—without a blot!
O, let me have thee whole,—all,—all—be mine!
    That shape, that fairness, that sweet minor zest
Of love, your kiss, those hands, those eyes divine,
8   That warm, white, lucent, million-pleasured breast,—
Yourself—your soul—in pity give me all,
    Withhold no atom's atom or I die,
Or living on perhaps, your wretched thrall,
12   Forget, in the mist of idle misery,
Life's purposes,—the palate of my mind
Losing its gust, and my ambition blind.

Sources and Notes

SOURCES

Bate	Bate, Walter Jackson. *John Keats.* Cambridge: Belknap Press of Harvard University Press, 1963.
Clarke	Clarke, Charles and Mary Cowden. *Recollections of Writers.* London: Sampson Low, Marston, Searle, and Rivington, 1878. Reprinted as "Recollections of John Keats." *Rare Early Essays on John Keats.* Edited by Carmen Joseph Dello Buono. Derby, PA: Norwood Editions, 1980.
Kandl	Kandl, John. "The Politics of Keats's Early Poetry." *The Cambridge Companion to Keats.* Edited by Susan J. Wolfson. Cambridge: Cambridge University Press, 2001.
Stillinger	Keats, John. *Complete Poems.* Edited by Jack Stillinger. Cambridge: Belknap Press of Harvard University Press, 1982.
Wordsworth	Wordsworth, William. *The Letters of William and Dorothy Wordsworth: The Later Years.* Edited by Ernest de Selincourt. 3 vols. Oxford: The Clarendon Press, 1939.
Letters	Keats, John. *The Letters of John Keats.* Edited by Hyder Edward Rollins. 2 vols. Cambridge: Harvard University Press, 1958.

The text of the sonnets, dates of composition, and information about first publication come from John Keats, *Complete Poems,* edited by Jack Stillinger.

NOTES (listed by sonnet number)

No. 2. *he had written it:* Stillinger, p. 418, citing Richard Woodhouse ms. note.

No. 5. *the first proof:* Clarke, p. 61.

No. 7. *soul as distinguished:* Letters, II, no. 159. Keats to the George Keatses, April 21, 1819.

No. 9. *a beastly place:* Letters, I, no. 7. Keats to Charles Cowden Clarke, October 9, 1816.

No. 12. *among the English Poets:* Letters, I, no. 120. Keats to the George Keatses, October 14, 1818.

No. 17. *his delighted stares:* Clarke, p. 64.

No. 18. *Keats was suddenly:* Clarke, pp. 66–67.

No. 22. *Last Evening:* Letters, I, no. 11.
The Idea: Letters, I, no. 12. November 21, 1816.
The sonnet appears: Wordsworth, pp. 1367–68.
to restore the same: Kandl, p. 1, quoting Leigh Hunt, "Young Poets," *The Examiner,* December 1, 1816.

No. 24. *favorite Speculation:* Letters, I, no. 43. Keats to Benjamin Bailey, November 22, 1817.

No. 25. *Written in 15 minutes:* Stillinger, p. 426, citing note of Tom Keats's on the original draft.

No. 26. *Keats won:* Clarke, p. 70.

No. 29. *I hope Apollo:* Letters, I, no. 38. October 8, 1817.
a test, a trial: Ibid.
The Imagination: Letters, I, no. 43. Keats to Bailey, November 22, 1817.

No. 31. *another example:* Clarke, p. 73.

No. 32 *forthwith . . . withdrew:* Clarke, pp. 71–72.

No. 33. *two noble sonnets:* Letters, I, no. 15. Haydon to Keats, March 3, 1817.

No. 35. *I believe it was:* Stillinger, p. 428, citing Woodhouse ms. note.

No. 37. *into the country:* Letters, I, no. 18. Keats to J. H. Reynolds, March 17, 1817.
a trial of my: Letters, I, no. 38. Keats to Bailey (quoting a lost letter to George Keats), October 8, 1817.
I have been rather narvus: Letters, I, no. 22. April 17, 1817.

No. 40. *felt the greatness:* Letters, I, no. 55. January 23, 1818.
a little change: Letters, I, no. 56. January 23, 1818.

No. 41. *serious poetical letter:* Letters, I, no. 58
As to what you say: Letters, I, no. 38.

No. 42. *for some few moments:* Stillinger, p. 438, citing Woodhouse ms. note.
Keats mentioned: Bate, p. 36, n. 15.

No. 43. *ready within the time:* Stillinger, p. 438, citing Woodhouse ms. note.

No. 45. The reference is to Stillinger, p. 439.

No. 46. *an old Comparison:* Letters, I, no. 62.

No. 47. *may be carried:* Letters, I, no. 67.

No. 50. *this Sonnet:* Letters, I, no. 93. July 1, 1818.
One of the pleasantest: Letters, I, no. 96. July 11, 1818.

No. 51. *I shall endeavour:* Letters, I, no. 97.

No. 52. *We went to the Cottage:* Letters, I, no. 96. July 13, 1818.
I was determined: Letters, I, no. 97. July 10, 1818.

No. 53. *the woods seem old:* Letters, I, no. 98. July 18, 1818.

No. 54. *went up Ben Nevis:* Letters, I, no. 101. August 3, 1818.
sat on the stones: Stillinger, p. 450, citing Charles Brown, *Life of John Keats.*

No. 55. *Gorge the honey:* Letters, I, no. 108.

No. 56. *I am ever afraid:* Letters, II, no. 159. March 19, 1819.

No. 57. *The fifth canto:* Letters, II, no. 159. April 16, 1819.

No. 59. *some of my old sins:* Letters, II, no. 159. April 30, 1819.

No. 62. *I have been endeavouring:* Letters, II, no. 159. May 3, 1819.

No. 63. The reference is to Stillinger, p. 479.
O my love: Letters, II, no. 182. August 16, 1819.

Appendix: Rhyme Schemes of Keats's Sonnets

Adapted from "John Keats: Perfecting the Sonnet" in Coming of Age as a Poet *by Helen Vendler (Harvard University Press, 2003)*

SONNET TYPES, CLASSIFIED BY RHYME SCHEME

In the case of a longer line, the number of feet is specified in subscript after the affected line number: e.g., 14_6 indicates a final hexameter. Rhyme schemes are in standard type. Rhyme *units* such as quatrains or tercets or couplets are underlined as they occur in Keats's octaves and sestets. They help to identify the differing components of the Keatsian sestet.

Regular Types

P = Petrarchan: abba abba octave, plus sestet, classified by the form of the sestet.

P_1 = cde cde (two rhyming tercets).
6 sonnets: Nos. 10, 12, 19, 26, 30, 38

P_2 = Shakespearean quatrain, plus . . .

P_{2a} = cdcd cd (Shakespearean quatrain plus continued rhyme)
22 sonnets: Nos. 2, 3, 4, 5, 6, 7, 8, 11, 17, 18, 20, 21, 23, 28, 29, 32, 33, 34, 36, 39, 43, 51

P_{2a+} = cdcd cd with 14_6
1 sonnet: No. 13

P_{2a-} = cdcd [c-] d: shortened 5th line, unrhymed
1 sonnet: No. 22

P_{2b} = cdcd dc (Shakespearean quatrain plus reversed rhyme)
1 sonnet: No. 25

P_3 = Petrarchan quatrain, plus . . .

P_{3a} = cddc dc (Petrarchan quatrain plus reversed rhyme)
2 sonnets: Nos. 9, 16

P_{3b} = cddc ee (Petrarchan quatrain plus Shakespearean couplet)
1 sonnet: No. 31

P_4 = c dede c (bracketed quatrain)
4 sonnets: Nos. 14, 35, 37, 50

P_5 = (sestet contains no quatrain)
2 sonnets: Nos. 24 [cdedce], 27 [cdefdf]

Total Petrarchan: 40

S = Shakespearean (three alternately-rhymed quatrains plus couplet)

S = Regular Shakespearean sonnet
14 sonnets: Nos. 41, 42, 44, 45, 47, 48, 49, 52, 54, 56, 58, 60, 63, 64

S_+ = Shakespearean sonnet with 14_6
1 sonnet: No. 57

Total Shakespearean: 15
Total of Regular Sonnets: 55

Anomalous Types

H = Hybrid. Three types:

H_P = Petrarchan octave with Shakespearean sestet [cdcd ee]
2 sonnets: Nos. 15, 53

H_{P+} = Petrarchan octave with Shakespearean sestet having 14_6
1 sonnet: No. 40

H_{S++} = Shakespearean octave with Petrarchan sestet [dd ed ee] having 9_7 and 14_6
1 sonnet: No. 1

Total Hybrid: 4

I = Irregularly rhymed sonnet. Three types:
3 sonnets: No. 59: Shakespearean octave with sestet bc efef
No. 61: Shakespearean octave with sestet efe gg f
No. 62: abc ab (d) c abc dede (tercets, quatrain)

U = Unrhymed sonnet
1 sonnet: No. 46

D = Douzain reduced in translation from French sonnet
1 sonnet: No. 55

Total Other: 5
Total Anomalous: 9
Grand Total, Regular and Anomalous: 64

RHYME SCHEMES OF THE 64 SONNETS

No. 1. On Peace
H_{S++}: Hybrid: S octave, P sestet [dd ed ee], with 9_7 and 14_6

No. 2. As from the darkening gloom a silver dove
P_{2a} : Petrarchan with cdcd cd

No. 3. To Lord Byron
P_{2a} : Petrarchan with cdcd cd

No. 4. Oh Chatterton! how very sad thy fate
P_{2a} : Petrarchan with cdcd cd

No. 5. Written on the Day That Mr. Leigh Hunt Left Prison
P_{2a} : Petrarchan with cdcd cd

No. 6. Woman! when I behold thee flippant, vain
P_{2a} : Petrarchan with cdcd cd

No. 7. Light feet, dark violet eyes, and parted hair
P_{2a} : Petrarchan with cdcd cd

No. 8. Ah! Who can e'er forget so fair a being?
P_{2a}: Petrarchan with cdcd cd

No. 9. O Solitude! if I must with thee dwell
P_{3a}: Petrarchan with cddc dc

No. 10. Had I a man's fair form, then might my sighs
P_{1}: Petrarchan with cde cde

No. 11. To one who has been long in city pent
P_{2a}: Petrarchan with cdcd cd

No. 12. Oh! how I love, on a fair summer's eve
P_{1}: Petrarchan with cde cde

No. 13. To a Friend Who Sent Me Some Roses
P_{2a+}: Petrarchan with cdcd cd and 14_6

No. 14. Happy is England! I could be content
P_{4}: Petrarchan with c dede c

No. 15. To My Brother George
H_{p}: Hybrid: P octave, S sestet [cdcd ee]

No. 16. How many bards gild the lapses of time
P_{3a}: Petrarchan with cddc dc

No. 17. On First Looking into Chapman's Homer
P_{2a}: Petrarchan with cdcd cd

No. 18. Keen, fitful gusts are whisp'ring here and there
P_{2a}: Petrarchan with cdcd cd

No. 19. On Leaving Some Friends at an Early Hour
P_{1}: Petrarchan with cde cde

No. 20. To My Brothers
P_{2a}: Petrarchan with cdcd cd

No. 21. Addressed to Haydon
P_{2a}: Petrarchan with cdcd cd

No. 22. Addressed to the Same
P_{2a-}: Petrarchan with cdcd [c-] d (shortened 5th line)

No. 23. To G. A.W.
P_{2a}: Petrarchan with cdcd cd

No. 24. To Kosciusko
P_{5}: Petrarchan with cdedce (no quatrain or tercets)

No. 25. Written in Disgust of Vulgar Superstition
P_{2b}: Petrarchan with cdcd dc

No. 26. On the Grasshopper and Cricket
P_{1}: Petrarchan with cde cde

No. 27. After dark vapours have oppressed our plains
P_{5}: Petrarchan with cdefdf (no quatrain or tercets)

No. 28. To a Young Lady Who Sent Me a Laurel Crown
P_{2a}: Petrarchan with cdcd cd

No. 29. On Receiving a Laurel Crown from Leigh Hunt
P_{2a}: Petrarchan with cdcd cd

No. 30. To the Ladies Who Saw Me Crown'd
P_{1}: Petrarchan with cde cde

No. 31. This pleasant tale is like a little copse
P_{3b}: Petrarchan with cddc ee

No. 32. To Leigh Hunt, Esq.
P_{2a}: Petrarchan with cdcd cd

No. 33. On Seeing the Elgin Marbles
P_{2a}: Petrarchan with cdcd cd

No. 34. To Haydon with a Sonnet Written on Seeing the Elgin Marbles
P_{2a}: Petrarchan with cdcd cd

No. 35. On a Leander Which Miss Reynolds, My Kind Friend, Gave Me
P_{4}: Petrarchan with c dede c

No. 36. On *The Story of Rimini*
P_{2a}: Petrarchan with cdcd cd

No. 37. On the Sea
P_{4}: Petrarchan with c dede c

No. 38. Before he went to live with owls and bats
P_{1}: Petrarchan with cde cde

No. 39. To Mrs. Reynolds's Cat
P_{2a}: Petrarchan with cdcd cd

No. 40. On Sitting Down to Read *King Lear* Once Again
H_{P+}: Hybrid: P octave with S sestet having 14_6

No. 41. When I have fears that I may cease to be
S: Shakespearean

No. 42. Time's sea hath been five years at its slow ebb
S: Shakespearean

No. 43. To the Nile
P_{2a}: Petrarchan with cdcd cd

No. 44. Spenser, a jealous honorer of thine
S: Shakespearean

No. 45. Blue!—'Tis the life of heaven—the domain
S: Shakespearean

No. 46. O thou whose face hath felt the winter's wind
U: Unrhymed, but sense units are two end-stopped quatrains, an end-stopped couplet, and a final quatrain, therefore tending toward Shakespearean form

No. 47. Four seasons fill the measure of the year
S: Shakespearean

No. 48. To J. R.
S: Shakespearean

No. 49. To Homer
S: Shakespearean

No. 50. On Visiting the Tomb of Burns
P_4: Petrarchan with c dede c

No. 51. To Ailsa Rock
P_{2a}: Petrarchan with cdcd cd

No. 52. This mortal body of a thousand days
S: Shakespearean

No. 53. Of late two dainties were before me plac'd
H_P: Hybrid: Petrarchan octave with Shakespearean sestet

No. 54. Read me a lesson, Muse, and speak it loud
S: Shakespearean

No. 55. Nature withheld Cassandra in the skies
D: Douzain, rhyming irregularly abab caca dede, therefore closer to Shakespearean model, although French original is Petrarchan

No. 56. Why did I laugh tonight? No voice will tell
S: Shakespearean

No. 57. As Hermes once took to his feathers light
S_+: Shakespearean with 14_6

No. 58. Bright star, would I were stedfast as thou art
S: Shakespearean

No. 59. Sonnet to Sleep
I: Irregularly rhymed with S octave: abab cdcd bc efef

No. 60. On Fame
S: Shakespearean

No. 61. On Fame (II)
I: Irregularly rhymed with S octave: abab cdcd efe gg f

No. 62. If by dull rhymes our English must be chain'd
I: Irregularly rhymed: abc ad (d) c abc dede (tercets, quatrain)

No. 63. The day is gone, and all its sweets are gone
S: Shakespearean

No. 64. I cry your mercy—pity—love!—aye, love
S: Shakespearean

Index of Titles and First Lines